Stop Stealing Sheep

"This does an excellent job of explaining modern typographic thinking to the uneducated user of type. It serves to open up the craft and language of type to a wider audience."
Neville Brody, Jury Panel Member
The 100 Show, 1994 Design Year in Review

"The most intellectually stimulating book on type recently…While essentially a user's guide to typographic aesthetics in the computer age, it is also the first philosophical tract on contemporary practice."
AIGA Journal of Graphic Design

"If you're mystified by the title, *Stop Stealing Sheep & find out how type works,* you need this book. This spirited guide to typography will help novice as well as expert type users decipher unfamiliar terminology and rules."
MacUser Magazine

"It is clear that much thought and planning has gone into this book, for beneath its attractive and engaging surface lays a wealth of typographic knowledge, advice, and wisdom that readers will absorb without feeling they are being lectured."
Letter Arts Review

"A gentle little introduction to a field, publishing, into which the computer has dropped a lot of unsuspecting souls in the last few years."
New York Times

Stop Stealing Sheep

& find out how type works

Erik Spiekermann
& E.M. Ginger

Adobe Press
Mountain View
California
1993

Library of Congress Catalog No.: 92-76016

ISBN: 0-672-48543-5

First Printing: December 1992
10 9 8 7 6 5 4 3 2

Printed in the United States of America. Published simultaneously in Canada.

Adobe Press books are published and distributed by Hayden, a division of Prentice Hall Computer Publishing.

For sales, and corporate sales accounts, call 1-800-428-5331
For information, address Hayden, 201 W. 103rd Street, Indianapolis, IN 46290, or call 317-581-3718.

Stealing sheep? Letterspacing lower case? Professionals in all trades, whether they be dentists, carpenters, or nuclear scientists, communicate in languages that seem secretive and incomprehensible to outsiders; type designers and typographers are no exception. Typographic terminology sounds cryptic enough to put off anyone but the most hard-nosed typomaniac. The aim of this book is to clarify the language of typography for people who want to communicate more effectively with type.

These days people need better ways to communicate to more diverse audiences. We know from experience that what we have to say is much easier for others to understand if we put it in the right voice; type is that voice, the visible language linking writer and reader. With thousands of typefaces available, choosing the right one to express even the simplest idea is bewildering to most everyone but practiced professionals.

Familiar images are used in this book to show that typography is not an art for the chosen few, but a powerful tool for anyone who has something to say and needs to say it in print. You will have ample opportunity to find out why there are so many typefaces, how they ought to be used, and why more of them are needed every day.

This is a sidebar. As you can see by the small type, the copy in here is not for the faint of heart, nor for the casual reader. All the information that might be a little heady for novices is put in this narrow column; it is, however, right at hand when they become infected by their first attacks of typomania.

For those who already know something about type and typography and who simply want to check some facts, read some gossip, and shake their heads at our opinionated comments, this is the space to watch.

In 1936, Frederic Goudy was in New York City to receive an award for excellence in type design. Upon accepting a certificate, he took one look at it and declared that "Anyone who would letterspace black letter would steal sheep." This was an uncomfortable moment for the man sitting in the audience who had hand lettered the award certificate. Mr. Goudy later apologized profusely, claiming that he said that about everything.

You might have noticed that our book cover reads "lower case," while here it reads "black letter" – two very different things. Lower case letters, as opposed to CAPITAL LETTERS, are what you are now reading; black letter isn't seen very often and looks like this.

We're not sure how "black letter" got changed to "lower case," but we've always known it to be the latter; whichever way, it makes infinite sense. By the time you finish this book we hope you will understand and be amused by Mr. Goudy's pronouncement.

PAUL WATZLAWICK

You cannot *not* communicate.

Paul Watzlawick (1921–)
is author of *Pragmatics of
Human Communication*, a
book about the influence of
media on peoples' behavior.
"You cannot *not* communicate"
is known as Watzlawick's First
Axiom of Communication.

CHAPTER 1

Type is everywhere

Have you ever been to Japan? A friend who went there recently reported that he had never felt so lost in his life. Why? Because he could not read anything: not road signs, not price tags, not instructions of any kind. It made him feel stupid, he said. It also made him realize how much we all depend on written communication.

Picture yourself in a world without type. True, you could do without some of the ubiquitous advertising messages, but you wouldn't even know which package on your breakfast table contained what.

Sure enough, there are pictures on them – grazing cows on a paper carton suggest that milk is inside, and cereal packaging has appetizing images to make you hungry. But pick up salt or pepper, and what do you look for? S and P!

Works in most languages, avoiding tasteless mistakes: S for Salt and P for Pepper.

Try to find your way around without type and you'll be as lost as most of us would be in Japan, where there is plenty of type to read, but only for those who have learned to read the right sort of characters.

You've hardly got your eyes open when you have to digest your first bite of type. How else would you know how much calcium fits on your spoon?

Breakfast for some people wouldn't be the same without the morning paper. And here it is again: inevitable type. Most people call it "print" and don't pay too much attention to typographic subtleties. You've probably never compared the small text typefaces in different newspapers, but you do know that some newspapers are easier to read than others. It might be because they have larger type, better pictures, and lots of headings to guide you through the stories. Regardless, all these differences are conveyed by type. In fact, a newspaper gets its look, its personality, from the typefaces used and how they are arranged on the page.

Type can say a lot more about a newspaper than just the information it carries.

We easily recognize our favorite newspapers on the newsstand, even if we only see the edge of a page, just as we recognize our friends by seeing only their hands or their hair. And just as people look different across the world, so do the newspapers in different countries. What looks totally unacceptable to a North American reader will please the French reader at breakfast, while an Italian might find a German daily paper too monotonous.

Of course, it's not only type or layout that distinguishes newspapers, it is also the combination of words. Some languages have lots of accents, like French; some have very long words, like Dutch or Finnish; and some use extremely short ones, as in a British tabloid. Not every typeface is suited for every language, which also explains why certain type styles are popular in certain countries, but not necessarily anywhere else.

What appears frightfully complex and incomprehensible to people who have learned to read only the Latin alphabet brings news to the majority of the world's population. Chinese and Arabic are spoken by more than half the people on this planet.

Some of the accents, special signs, and characters used in languages other than English, giving each of them its unique appearance.

13

ourier only a guest : Becker's feast

ine in Frankfurt

SOME it was an pset; to Jim Courier it as more of a confirma-on. Though now the ed No. 1 in the men's e American had never oris Becker and yester-uffered his sixth loss to an.

his latest defeat, in the the £1.3 million ATP hampionship here, the n also admitted: "He's ma fair and square ne."

a fitting outcome for t professional match had ever been called play on his birthday, this is your day," ed one of the many s draped from the balconies, and so it

rman won 6–4, 6–3, 7–5 23min, having rather difficulty blowing out adles on his birthday n he had in dampening n fire.

Becker entered the en three weeks ago he an outside chance of alifying for the eight-try to this prestigious l event. Now he has be-first man to win it in inents.

evious victory was in een defeated Ivan arden. He won then on ord, and yesterday the n came to his aid on at occasions. If it was day it certainly was ter's.

whose late surge has m back to No. 5 in the s, says he now has his t on being No. 1 again. on fast carpet courts, tainly has no peer. half his victories in 1992 me indoors, whereas on

grass, cement and clay his achievements have been mod-est. Courier, by contrast, is at his best with the sun on his back, and he will not give up his hard-won position easily.

The trouble always with Becker is that his enthusiasm comes in fits and starts. Since the start of the Paris tourna-ment, which he won with some of his most brilliant tennis, he has looked near his best. Yet he is not due to play again for six weeks, having declined an invi-tation to next month's Grand Slam Cup in Munich. Reports that this was because he was soon to be married were dis-missed by Becker. "That's rub-bish," he said.

A six-week break may well test his enthusiasm, and he returns in Qatar in a strong field which includes Goran Ivanisevic and Stefan Edberg, both of whom he beat to reach yesterday's final.

Saturday's match with the Croat was described by their manager Ion Tiriac as "the best of the decade".

It was certainly a riveting contest, with Becker serving su-perbly throughout, and that may have accounted for the fact that his service against Courier yesterday was noticeably less lethal. With 8,500 fans behind him, however, Becker was al-ways able to dig deep enough to find the right shot when it mattered.

It was not a pitiful affair. Indeed, in more than two hours' play only three rallies went into double figures. Most points were settled by a serve, a volley and — in Courier's case — a passing shot from the baseline.

Had the American scored more of these winners the match might have gone to a fourth set — and that would have been intriguing, as Becker was showing signs of fatigue as the curtain fell.

Victory earned Becker $1.09 million (about £720,000), more than doubling his earnings for the year. Courier also lifted his annual total above $2 million but he said he was now ready for a rest and would prefer to play only doubles for the United States in their Davis Cup final against Switzerland next month.

The final was 10 minutes old before a point was won against either server. At 3–3, however, Courier double-faulted at 40–15, let Becker back to deuce with a backhand error and then con-ceded break point when he let go a return which just nicked the sideline. Seeing his opening, Becker exploded a backhand winner off the back foot that left Courier helpless.

It was the same story in the second set. Again at 3–3 Courier failed to withstand the pres-sure, dropping his serve to love, and Becker was rampant in es-tablishing a two-set lead.

The third was more even, each in turn having a break be-fore the score reached 4–4. At 5–5 it was Becker's turn to fight for survival, but he came up with two huge serves — the second being his 14th ace of the match — and attacked Courier with sufficient venom at 6–5 to force him into double-faulting to concede double match point. On the second Courier fired a backhand wide off a great return and the crowd rose to a chorus of Happy Birthday.

A delighted Becker said it was great to have beaten the world's No. 4, No. 2 and No. 1. In a row: "It means that for this evening at least I feel like I'm the No. 1." If he continued to play his best, he felt, the No. 1 position would surely be his again.

FINAL 1992 ATP RANKINGS: 1, J Courier (US); 2, S Edberg (Swe); 3, P Sampras (US); 4, G Ivanisevic (Croatia); 5, B Becker (Ger); 6, M Chang (US); 7, P Korda (Cz); 8, I Lendl (US); 9, A Agassi (US); 10, R Krajicek (Netherlands).

Birthday treat . . . Boris Becker was 25 yesterday and the world No. 1 Jim Courier could not hold a candle to him in the ATP final PHOTOGRAPH: JOACHIM

---

es Bitter Championship: Salford 18, Wigan 26

igan keep their nerve

zpatrick

LFORD have not opped Wigan winning e cups and the champ-but they have had the on of setting some em-ng ambushes for the n ross Central Park.

beat them twice last and looked as though ght achieve the unex-again yesterday at The s when they went into a a after only 10 minutes might have been enough oralise other sides, but are not champions for . By half-time they had the deficit to four nd at the end, on a pitch 1 to tire the strongest ey were in undisputed

d's best crowd of the had no right to expect ility that was sustained cious conditions. There mistakes, but the pace lented, the skill and ment never faltered.

Wigan suffered a nervous start and Salford twice made pay for their blunders. First Offiah allowed himself to be bundled into touch on the second tackle and after winning the scrum Coleman put Bleasdale into a gap which he exploited to the full. Then Stoop, forgetting in the conditions, fumbled Lee's angled kick and Bradshaw came sliding in for the second try. Blakeley, who had left Wigan for The Willows on Thursday, improved both feet and Wigan were floundering.

The introduction of Sam Pan-apa for the vulnerable Stoop was one reason for Wigan's im-provement; Salford's increas-ing tendency to err was an-other, and gradually Wigan chipped away at the lead.

After Wigan had won a scrum, Bell took advantage of Gibson's hesitancy and neatly sidestepped his opponent before scoring the 9th try of his career. Botica, who earlier landed a penalty, improved the touchdown and the deficit was now only four points.

Wigan were unlucky not to take the lead six minutes later when Offiah, put through by the influential Edwards, burst clear only to be brought back, the pass ruled forward. But they were now well into their stride.

An exchange of passes be-tween Offiah and Farrar on the left brought a try for the trans-fer-listed Lucas soon after half-time, and then came the best score of the game when the out-standing Panapa burst on to Bell's short, perfectly timed pass and ran 70 yards to the line.

Salford were not done, as Gil-fillan proved with a determined try eight minutes from time. But Wigan finished powerfully, with Betts scoring from close range and Botica landing his fifth goal from six attempts.

SALFORD: Gibson (Fairclough, 80min); Evans, Crompton, Gilfillan, Coleman; Blakely, Coleman; Young, Lee, Blatcher (Reid, 55), Bradshaw, Hosea (Dunn, 60). **Tries:** Bleasdale, Bradshaw, Gilfillan. **Goals:** Panapa, 3.
WIGAN: Stoop (Panapa, 26); Lydon, Bell, Farrar, Offiah; Edwards, Bell; Lucas, Dermott, Platt, Betts, McGinty (Cowie, 26), Clarke.
Referee: R Smith (Castleford).

12, Leeds 12

bson reduces the blushes

uxley

ITHER Leigh nor Leeds ill have been happy ith a share of the points on Park yesterday be-heir Stones Bitter Cham-p positions are increas-erious. Both are in the three.

will probably be the pleased; the yield of a more encouragement in truggle to climb away a foot.

, more desperate with passing week, started style and determination ggested they might be reach of their first away the season, but three fac-e expectation sink grad-nto the gluttonous sur-ury failed to adapt their ng to the conditions, ck could not subdue the Leigh six and their

game plan lacked cohesion and application.

In the end it took a 76th-min-ute try by their former Great Britain centre Carl Gibson to spare them the embarrassment of an eighth successive away defeat. They have won only six league games since last sea-son's Regal Trophy final.

Leigh had been leading 12–8 and, after controlling the ball for long periods in the second half, would have been worthy winners. Since the arrival of their coach Steve Simms from South Sydney they have shown signs of an application that could eventually save them.

Leeds's fast-passing style was never going to suit the condi-tions, although it did produce their first try in the ninth min-ute after a four-man move out the second-row forward Paul art Pugsley, with David Tanner

adding the goal. But Leeds won, in at half-time with the lead after the winger Jim Fallon had gone over for their second touchdown in the 23rd minute.

A slice of fortune presented Leigh's substitute Simon Bald-win with a 58th-minute try. Baldwin, a 17-year-old member of the club's academy team who was making his senior debut, dribbled through a loose ball that had rebounded from a Leeds player and touched down. Tanner kicked the goal.

That gave Leigh the lead and they never looked like losing it until Gibson broke away to run half the length of the field. John Gallagher, needing to add the goal points to win the match, fell short.

LEIGH: Tanner; Ledger, D Pearce, Mabon, Hill; Donohue, Pugsley; Hansen (Martin, 49min), A Ruane, Costello (Baldwin, 49), Elias, Collier, Pendlebury.
LEEDS: Gallagher; Fallon, Iro, Innes, Gibson; Schofield, Irwin; Molloy, Lowes, Nine, Goodway, Dixon (O'Neill, 5-6), Hanley.
Referee: J Holdsworth (Kippax).

st

CK FOX, the Brad-l Northern second-uled himself out of d's team for Friday's onal against Wales

side's way on 28 minutes when Ropati touched down after Powell made a hash of a clearance.

Fallon held on to bear Warrington 21–20 in a Thrum Hall thriller. War-rington scored four tries to

the scrum after 18 minutes to set up Smith for a try which Crooks converted and a Crooks penalty made it 8–0. Sheffield Eagles produced a powerful second-half dis-

---

Davis returns to his flawless best

Clive Everton

STEVE DAVIS'S appetite for the game was unaf-fected by his decline from first to fourth in the world rankings. His enjoy-ment of it was keener than ever as he sensed a sustained restoration of much of his old form and the possibility of a seventh Royal Liver As-surance UK Championship.

Having dropped only one frame in his first two matches, he yesterday des-patched the world No. 10 Steve James 9–4. "When I've been presented with chances in this tournament I haven't let many go," he said, after breaks of 81, 63, 105 and 79.

James either showed his talents too late, making breaks of 56, 62 and 132 in recovering from 2–8 to 4–8, or ruined his hard work with errors. In four consecutive frames from 1–2 he missed when in play with 30 or so, and he won only one of them.

John Parrott, the defend-ing champion and Davis's prospective semi-final oppo-nent, leads Dean Reynolds 7–1. Reynolds, out of sorts and sometimes too venture-some, was so disgusted by missing the penultimate red in the fifth that he conceded, only 15 behind, rather than wait for a less than inevita-ble executioner's axe.

He won the sixth with a

break of 64 and led by 48 in the seventh, only for Parrott to win it with 53 and a brown-to-pink clearance. Even more gallingly, Reyn-olds put the world No. 2 in after a foul in the last frame of the day and saw Parrott pot the last red from distance and clear with 31 to win on the black.

Stephen Hendry, attempt-ing to win his third UK title in four years, despatched Cliff Wilson 9–3 after seizing a 7–1 interval lead. The world champion made a break of 118 and eight half-centuries in a superb after-noon display.

Though admitting that dur-ing that session Hendry had been unstoppable, Wilson of-fered his thoughts on the Scot's recent inconsistency. "He's putting too much pres-sure on himself. He needs to relax. He's playing every frame as if his life depended on it. I've never seen him as uptight as he was today."

Jimmy White, winner of last month's Rothmans Grand Prix, earned a 6–2 in-terval lead over Willie Thorne, who had beaten him in the Dubai Classic. Breaks of 89, 98, 53 and 63 by White and 81 by Thorne were largely responsible for a 4–1 scoreline.

At 5–5, Thorne led 44–0 but missed the simplest of reds and lost the frame to White's 68.

Britons scale early pea

Mike Greasley

A WORLD championship may be at stake but for tens of thousands of fans who yesterday braved appall-ing weather on the opening day of the 1,500-mile Lombard RAC Rally attention was focused on a stirring battle for British hon-our. At times its intensity even threatened to overwhelm the rally and world championship leader Carlos Sainz in his Toyota.

Although the 30-year-old Spaniard returned to Chester last night with a 35sec lead over the Italian Miki Biasion in a Ford, Colin McRae's third place, only four seconds ahead of Malcolm Wilson, gave the rain-soaked fans something to cheer about.

McRae has been able to underline his considerable tal-ent with impressive results both at home and on world championship rallies in Sweden, Greece and Finland this year. In complete contrast Wilson has been busy develop-ing Ford's new rally challenger, which has kept him out of the limelight.

Second and third after four

stages in Wales, the Lake Dis-trict and Scotland. Often in the past it has been lost over the deceptive artificial special stages which are run as crowd pleasers at race circuits and stately homes.

Both McRae and Wilson seemed at times to be in danger of forgetting that these opening stages rarely reflect a true pic-ture of this final round in the world rally championship.

Wilson, from Cumbria, is 36 and on his last world champion-ship rally as a Ford factory driver. He has largely been ig-nored in the pre-rally hype which has surrounded McRae, aged 24, the Rothmans Subaru driver and newly crowned Brit-ish champion.

As the 158 starters from 13 countries slipped and slid their way over yesterday's treacher-ous nine stages, most had the thought uppermost in their mind that this was only a pre-lude to the real business. The RAC will be run over the next three days of gravel forestry

special stages, Wil Whitbread of the two-pitch East Regional Hockey Centre.

Hounslow deserved their win after Gladman had skilfully given Loughborians the lead, but were grateful to Nick Thompson, Loughborians' in-ternational forward, for wast-ing a late penalty stroke won by Julian Halls. Both Hounslow's goals, by Dave Hacker and Rob Crutchley, came from second-half corners.

The league champions Hav-ant continued their climb up the table with a Don Williams fine tickle in a 4–1 defeat of St Albans.

The outstanding scoring per-formance came from Reading, whose 9–0 win at Brean kept them on top of the Second Divi-sion. Paddy Osborn moved to the top of the league's goal-scorers' list with five goals, two of them field goals. He now has 11 goals, one more than Sher-ry's, Welch and Nick Thomp-son of the First Division.

In the women's National League Ipswich maintained a point advantage over Hightown with their first league win against their East rivals Chelmsford. With Sandy Lister, the England captain, running the game, Helen Bray (penalty stroke), Sarah Bamfield and their captain Debbie Rawlinson scored in a 3–1 victory over

---

Stourport slip up

Pat Rowley

STOURPORT dropped their first points of the season in a 2–2 draw at East Grinstead yesterday, but four points out of six in their two weekend games was enough to see them go to the top of the Pizza Express National League for the first time.

Only a late penalty-corner rebound goal by Jason Lee, Grinstead's Olympic winger, denied them two victories from their weekend in the south.

Stourport took over first place on Saturday with a 2–0 victory over Teddington. The team that beat them on penal-ties in the cup last season. Little was seen of the Teddington attack after Junott had gone close to equalising in the first half.

Dave Knott, as tenacious as ever, won a stroke converted by Imran Sherwani and scored Stourport's second after an ex-cellent attack. Knott then scored both goals yesterday to keep Stourport 2–1 ahead for most of the game at East Grinstead.

The Middlesex clubs South-gate and Hounslow cut Stour-port's lead to one point yester-day. Southgate went on the rampage against the promoted

---

Moore a Tower of strength as Cadle's Kings are thrown

Christian Bright

WHAT Joel Moore failed in experience to achieve for his country in midweek, he managed with spectacular suc-cess for his club last night.

To the chagrin of the England coach Kevin Cadle, Moore's match-winning contribution of 30 points for London Towers came against Cadle's club squad, the Guildford Kings, whose Carlsberg League title ambitions took a further dive.

Moore's fourth three-pointer of a stupendous game at the So-bell Centre came right on the final buzzer. It gave Towers vic-tory by 99–97 and completed a wretched week for Cadle and his five England internationals, all of whom had started despite an exhausting programme on behalf of country and club.

half, but a similar sequence by Towers yesterday precipitated their downfall.

Towers outscored the Kings 21–4 midway through the first half before Cadle's squad ral-lied to reduce their interval ar-rears to only five, 41–46.

Bailey hit 21 points and Rich-ard Scantlebury 20 for Towers, but the Kings appeared to have averted their fourth league de-feat of the season when Alton Byrd dragged them back from 96–92 down with five points in the last 23 seconds. Only four seconds remained when he sank a free throw to put the Kings up by 97–96.

Towers gave the ball to Moore and after taking aim from seemingly outrageous range just inside his own half he eased his own frustration, at least, for England's failure. He came up for air after being

---

Lim lays to the top

Richard Jago

LIM XIAOQUING Beijing to settl holm after the Square massacre ago, had special re pleased by her reti Glasgow Carlton Sc title yesterday wi 11–2 victory over Magnusson, also of the women's singles

Her success in th Prix event of the y the advantage wh dropped to fifth pla ing into straw ba Clumber Park stag losing 13 seconds t dent McRae was a back to third place, in front of Wilson, this opening leg fifth

McRae said: "My said that I had to porter's shed. Un they had moved the went straight into th Sainz, the overn was fastest on three terday, his nearest ship rival Juha trailing by 27 sec kunen, the outgo champion, was four stage in Birmingham

His Lancia team championship rival ried several tyres o McRae said: "My my new country's bid means a lot to me."

Pontus Jantti, won the men's sin enduring Darren Ha becoming the first to retain the title s against their East Chelmsford, with Sand score was 15–4, 15 former European rarely fitted hits g the game, Helen Bray heights he achieves the Danish Open

This brings us back to type and newspapers. What might look quite obvious and normal to you when you read your daily paper is the result of careful planning and applied craft. Even newspapers with pages that look messy are laid out following complex grids and strict hierarchies.

The artistry comes in offering the information in such a way that the reader doesn't get sidetracked into thinking about the fact that someone had to carefully prepare every line, paragraph, and column into structured pages. Design – in this case at least – has to be invisible. Typefaces used for these hardwork-

The Guardian, one of Britain's leading newspapers, is designed to a grid.

ing tasks are therefore by definition "invisible." They have to look so normal that you don't even notice you're reading them. And this is exactly why designing type is such an unknown profession; who thinks about people who produce invisible things? Nevertheless, every walk of life is defined by, expressed with, and indeed, dependent on type and typography.

Just as the newspaper on the opposite page is laid out according to an underlying structure of some intricacy, this book is designed within its own constraints.

The page is divided into equal parts, each of which has the same proportion as the whole page, i.e., 2:3. The page is made up of 144 rectangles, each one measuring 12 by 18 millimeters, 12 rectangles across and 12 down. This makes the page 144 by 216 millimeters, or roughly 5 $^{11}/_{16}$ by 8 $^{1}/_{2}$ inches. The columns are multiples of the 12-millimeter unit. Because there has to be some distance between columns, 3 mm (or more for wider columns) have to be subtracted from these multiples of 12 to arrive at the proper column width.

The distance between lines of type (still archaically referred to as *leading* [more about that later in the book]) is measured in multiples of 1.5 mm. All typographic elements are positioned on this baseline grid of 1.5 mm, which is fine enough to be all but invisible to the reader, but which helps layout and production. The discipline offered by a fine grid like this one gives the same sort of coherence to a page as bricks do to a building. They are small enough to allow for all styles of architecture, while serving as the common denominator for all other proportions.

15

If you think that the choice of a typeface is something of little importance because nobody would know the difference anyway, you'll be surprised to hear that experts spend an enormous amount of time and effort perfecting details that are invisible to the untrained eye.

It is a bit like having been to a concert, thoroughly enjoying it, then reading in the paper the next morning the conductor had been incompetent, the orchestra out of tune, and that the whole piece of music not worth performing in the first place. While you had a great night out, some experts were unhappy with the performance because their standards and expectations were different than yours.

The same thing happens when you have a glass of wine. While you might be perfectly happy with whatever you're drinking, someone at the table will make a face and go on at length why this particular bottle is too warm, how that year was a lousy one anyway, and that he just happens to have a case full of some amazing stuff at home that the uncle of a friend imports directly from France.

Does that make you a fool or does it simply say that there are varying levels of quality and satisfaction in everything we do?

Food and design: how often do we buy the typographic promise without knowing much about the product? Stereotypes abound – some colors suggest certain foods, particular typefaces suggest different flavors. Without these unwritten rules we wouldn't know what to buy or order.

As they say in England: "Different strokes for different folks."

The range of food and drink known to mankind is almost limitless. No single person could be expected to know them all. One guide through this maze of taste and nourishment, of sustenance as well as gluttony, is offered by the labels on products; as long as they are packaged in containers that can carry information. Without typography we wouldn't know which contains what or what should be used which way.

Small wonder that type on food packages is often hand lettered, because standard typefaces don't seem to be able to express this vast range of tastes and promises. Hand lettering these days sometimes means using software programs, like Adobe Illustrator, which combine design and artwork at a level unimaginable only a few years ago. Anything a graphic designer can think of can be produced in amazing quality.

Effects that mimic hand lettering, stone carving, and etching are all easily achieved electronically.

1993

Department of Fontography
Adobe Type Library

Instructions for Form TYPE4U
U.2. Can Add Emphasis To Words Through Type

(With help from Adobe Type Library)

Notice of History

When Gutenberg printed his forty-two-line Bible in 1456, he had only one typeface choice: the formal, square-text Gothic letter that mimicked the lettering of scribes. Who could have imagined typography would become so rich a resource for communication.

Today, designers and desktop publishers have tens of thousands of typefaces to choose from, and new designs are added continuously. To help make the job of selecting type easier, we have organized Adobe typefaces according to a simplified classification system. It is based on the internationally recognized system that has been adopted by the Association Typographique Internationale (ATypl), an organization that sets standards for the typographic industry. The British Standards Institution and the American National Standards Institute also have adopted this classification system.

When Gutenberg printed his forty-two-line Bible in 1456, he had only one typeface choice: the formal, square-text Gothic letter that mimicked the lettering of scribes. Who ~~could have~~ imagined typography would become so rich as a resource for com~~~~ desktop publishers have tens of thousands of t~~~~ ntinuously. To help ma~~~~

BARGAIN DOCTORS INC.
STATE OF THE ART
AFFORDABLE TREATMENT
999 HEADACHE PLACE
BROKEN LEG, INNER SPINE, IL 12345

APPLICATION FOR OPEN ACCOUNT

PANY NAME OR TRADE NAME				
RESS	STATE	ZIP	PHONE	
RS IN BUSINESS	AT ABOVE ADDRESS SINCE	NO. OF OUTLETS	BANKRUPTCY	YES NO
UNTS PAYABLE CONTACT		PHONE		
E OF OWNERSHIP	CORPORATION	PARTNERSHIP	PROPRIETORSHIP	

OWNERS, PARTNERS OR OFFICERS

ME	HOME ADDRESS	TITLE
ME	HOME ADDRESS	TITLE
ME	HOME ADDRESS	TITLE

BANK REFERENCES

NK	ADDRESS	ACCT NO.
NK	ADDRESS	ACCT NO.

TRADE REFERENCES

AME	ADDRESS	PHONE
AME	ADDRESS	PHONE

STATE OF CALIBRA SALES TAX EXEMPTION CERTIFICAT

WE CERTIFY THAT ALL MATERIAL, MERCHANDISE OR GOODS TO BE PURCHASED BY THE UNDER

IS FOR PURPOSE OF RESALE IN ITS ORIGINAL FORM. OUR PERMIT NO. IS

IS PART OF OR CONSUMED IN THE PRODUCTION OF A MANUFACTURED PRODUCT TO BE S OUR PERMIT NO. IS
IS OTHERWISE SALES TAX EXEMPT. PLEASE SPECIFY

Chang
•When Bible in choice: that mim could ha become

•Today, d have tens from, and continuous selecting t dobe type assificatio ternationa en adopti pographic anization ographic itution an dards In sification

en Guten in 1456, e: the for imicked have ima e so rich , designe thousan nd new c ously. To g type ea ypefaces ation sys nally rec pted by phique In ion that

---

WHILE YOU W

To	Date	Area code
From		
Of		Extension

URGENT! RETURNED CALL CALL BACK

REGISTERED NOTEPAD NO 1234567-89-0

WHILE YOU

To	Date	Area
From		
Of		Exten

URGENT! RETURNED CALL CALL BACK

REGISTERED NOTEPAD NO 1234567-89-0

URGENT! RETURNED CALL CALL BACK

REGISTERED NOTEPAD NO 1234567-89-0

6	2344	345	345	456	34	35
6	789	3345	561	123	12	56
5	2564	125	565	457	78	
6	2344	345	345	456	34	35
6	3421	323	789	456	32	78
8	9876	345	345	456	11	00
0	8944	045	005	156	34	35
6	2344	345	345	456	34	35
6	2344	345	345	456	34	35
6	789	3345	561	123	12	56
5	2564	125	565	457	78	
6	2344	345	345	456	34	35
6	3421	323	789	456	32	78
8	9876	345	345	456	11	00
0	8944	045	005	156	34	35
6	2344	345	345	456	34	35

Order Form

The Beehive Company ©

TM

P.O. Box 123
Nowheretown, CT 02361-5423

Please check your Address. We cannot ship to a P.O. Box

Ordered By:

Code: 234556
Sans Serif F.Rutiger
300 Rotis ST STE 8
New Jack City DC 92312-2345

EXTENDED ORDERING HOURS FROM 11/115 - 12/13!

DID YOU FORGET? Please check the follo

☐ Your Phone Number   ☐ Your Address (we cannot ship to P.O. Boxes

Credit Card Or

Monday thro
Saturdays 8

FAX Orders

Office use only

Phone Number:
Day ( )

Method of Paym
I wish to pay by

☐ Visa ☐ Mastercc

Issuing Bank No.

Expiration Date

Signature

Mastercard	Qty.	Description	Price Each	Total Price	Ship To Th

While it might be fun to look at wine labels, chocolate boxes, or candy bars in order to stimulate one's appetite for food or fonts (depending on your preference), most of us definitely do not enjoy an equally prevalent form of printed communication: forms.

If you think about it, you'll have to admit that business forms process a lot of information that would be terribly boring to have to write fresh every time. All you do is check a box, sign your name, and you get what you asked for. Unless, of course, you're filling out your tax return, when *they* get what they asked for. Or unless the form is so poorly written, designed, or printed (or all of the above) that you have a hard time understanding it. Given the typographic choices available, there is no excuse for producing bad business forms, illegible invoices, awkward applications, or ridiculous receipts. Not a day goes by without having to deal with printed matter of this nature. It could so easily be a more pleasant experience.

The "generic" look of all sorts of business forms is usually derived from technical constraints. But even when those restrictions no longer exist, the look lingers on, often confirming our prejudice against this sort of standardized communication.

Typefaces used for business communications have often been designed for a particular technology – optical character recognition, needle printers, monospaced typewriters, and other equipment.

What was once a technical constraint can today become a trend. The "nondesigned" look of OCR B, the good old honest typewriter faces, even the needle printer, or LCD (liquid crystal display) alphabets are being exploited by designers to evoke certain effects.

If you want to avoid any discussion about the typefaces you're using in your letters or invoices, you can fall back onto Courier, Letter Gothic, or other monospaced fonts (see page 115), even though they are less legible and take up more space than "proper" typefaces. You could be slightly more courageous and try one of those new designs that were created specifically to address both the question of legibility and space economy, and the readers' expectations.

Typefaces designed with technical constraints.

.Handgloves

LETTER GOTHIC

.Handgloves

COURIER

.Handgloves

OCR B

Some of the new typefaces designed to work well in business communication and on low-resolution output devices, such as laserprinters or ink-jet printers.

.Handgloves

ITC STONE INFORMAL

.Handgloves

LUCIDA

.Handgloves

ITC OFFICINA

E 5

4 Frankfurt

✈ 555

Köln Mitte
Köln Süd
555

Bonn
Rodenkirchen

350 m

Köln   Köln   Köln

A   B   C

Some of the most pervasive typographical messages have never really been designed, and neither have the typefaces that appear on them. Some engineer, administrator, or accountant in some government department had to decide what the signs on our roads and freeways should look like. This person probably formed a committee made up of other engineers, administrators, and accountants who in turn went to a panel of experts that would have included manufacturers of signs, road safety experts, lobbyists from automobile associations plus more engineers, administrators, and accountants. You can bet there wasn't one typographer or graphic designer in the group, so the outcome shows no indication of any thought toward legibility, let alone communication or beauty. Nevertheless we're stuck with our road signs. They dominate our open spaces, forming a large part of a country's visual culture.

The letterforms on these signs were constructed from simple geometric patterns rather than from written or drawn letterforms because they had to be re-created by signmakers all over the country. It seems our official alphabets are here to stay, even though it is feasible to use other typefaces more suitable for the task.

DIN (Deutsche Industrie-Norm= German Industrial Standard) is the magic word for anything that can be measured in Germany, including the official German typeface, appropriately (and not surprisingly) called DIN-Schrift. Since it's been available in digital form, this face has been picked up by many graphic designers who like it for its lean, geometric lines, features that don't make it the best choice for complex signage projects.

Signage systems have to fulfill complex demands. Reversed type (e.g., white type on a blue background) looks heavier than positive type (e.g., black on yellow), and back-lit signs have a different quality than front-lit ones. Whether you have to read a sign on the move (from a car, for example), or while standing still on a well-lit platform, or in an emergency – all these situations require careful typographic treatment. In the past these issues have been largely neglected, partly because it would have been almost impossible to implement and partly because designers chose to ignore these problems, leaving them up to other people who simply weren't aware that special typefaces could help improve the situation.

Multiple master typefaces (see pages 109–111) like Minion and Myriad can be tuned to every lighting condition and production specification. The PostScript™ data generated with these types in drawing and layout applications can be used to cut letters of any size from vinyl, metal, wood, or any other material used for signs.

Soon there will be no more excuses for badly designed signs, whether on our roads or inside our buildings.

A DIN-Schrift, reversed out.
B Type on back-lit sign suffers from radiant light.

C More explicit letter shapes help (o is more oval, i-dots are round).
D But still, backlighting presents a problem.

E The type has to be just a little lighter, so that finally…
F It is more legible than in example B.

D

E

F

There is less in this than
meets the eye.

Tallulah Bankhead (1903–1968)
was a celebrated international
actress and scandalous public
figure. Ms. Bankhead did all the
wrong things with consummate
flair and in the best of taste.

CHAPTER 2

What is type?

IMP CAE

TRAIAN

MAXIMO

ADDECLA

MONSETLO

13 A

Ever since people have been writing things down, they have had to consider their audience before actually putting pen to paper: letters would have to look different depending on whether they were to be read by many other people (in official documents or inscriptions), just one other person (in a letter), or only the writer (in a notebook or a diary). So there would be less room for guesswork, letter shapes were made more formal as the diversity of the readership expanded.

Some of the first messages to be read by a large number of people were rendered not by pens but by chisels. Large inscriptions on monuments in ancient Rome were carefully planned, with letters drawn on the stone with a brush before they were chiseled. Even if white-out had existed in those days, it would not have helped to remove mistakes made in stone. A bit of planning was also more important then, since stone masons were sometimes more expendable than slabs of marble or granite.

Graphic design and typography are complicated activities, but even simple projects benefit from thinking about the problem, forming a mental picture of the solution, and then carefully planning the production process.

SENATVS · POPVLVSQVE · ROMANVS

IMP · CAESARI · DIVI · NERVAE · F · NERVAE

TRAIANO · PRETTY · LEGIBLE · DACICON

MAXIMO · TRIB · POT · XVIII · IMP · VI · COS · VI · P · P

ADDECLARANDVM · VERY · SPACED · OUT

arboscelli, & di floride Geniste, & di multiplice herbe uerdissime, quiui
uidi il Cythiso, La Carice, la cómune Cerinthe. La muscariata Panachia
ria el fiorito ramunculo, & ceruicello, ouero Elaphio, & la seratula, & di
uarie assai nobile, & de molti altri proficui simplici, & ignote herbe & fio-
ri per gli prati dispensate. Tutta questa læta regione de uiridura copiosa-
mente adornata se offeriua. Poscia poco piu ultra del mediano suo io ri-
trouai uno sabuleto, ouero glareosa plagia, ma in alcuno loco dispersa-
mente cum alcuni cespugli de herbatura. Quiui al gliochii mei uno io-
cundissimo Palmeto se apresento cum le foglie di cultrato mucrone
ad táta utilitate ad gli ægyptii. del suo dulcissimo fructo fœcunde & abun
dante. Tra lequale racemose palme, & picole alcune, & molte mediocre,
& laltre drite erano & excelse, Electo Signo de uictoria per el resistere
suo ad lorgente pondo. Ancora & in questo loco non trouai incola, ne al
tro animale alcuno. Ma peregrinando solitario tra le non densate, ma in-
teruallate palme spectatissime, cogitando delle Rachelaide, Phaselide, &
Libyade, non essere forsa a queste comparabile. Echo che uno affermato
& carniuoro lupo alla parte dextera cum la bucca piena mi apparue.

In turn, these "official" styles of writing influenced how handwriting was looked at and how it was taught in schools or other learning centers, such as monasteries.

Today, when we are supposed to write legibly, we're instructed to "print." While we might have a hard time reading something written 200 years ago in what was then considered a

very "good" hand, we have no problem reading writing from Roman times or even earlier. Likewise, the typefaces designed 500 years ago, shortly after printing with movable type was invented, still look perfectly familiar (if a little quaint) to us. We might not be using the exact same letters reproduced in the identical manner, but the basic shapes and proportions are still valid today.

For centuries, *fraktur* (literally, "broken writing") was the standard typographic style in Northern Europe. Roman typefaces were called Roman because they came from Italy and were used to set Romance languages like Italian, French, and, of course, Latin.

When communications became more international, typefaces that were more universal came into demand. Today fraktur, gothic, and similar styles are only used to evoke the feeling of a bygone era, for example, on the banner of newspapers like *The New York Times.*

They also come in handy when someone has to design a job that has Germanic undertones. The Nazis did indeed sponsor and even order (as was their way) the use of what they called "Germanic" typefaces, making it impossible for generations after World War II to use these types without historical connotations.

Far left: Aldus Manutius' first type design, printed 1499. Bembo from the Monotype Corporation, 1929, the modern equivalent.
Left: Gutenberg's bible from 1455.

Some typefaces have stood the test of time and appear as contemporary today as they did 500 years ago. Their modern digitized versions have a slight edge when it comes to clean outlines.

Other typefaces were perfectly legible only a few decades ago, but can hardly be read by anybody today. It has to do with cultural perceptions, not the physical properties of the typefaces.

A chiunqe vole imparare scrivere tra
corsina, o sia Cancellaresca conviene

Primieramente'imparerai di fare' que=
sti dui tratti, cioe -'
dali quali se' principiano tutte'

Principē de eodem officio .   Corniculaxium .
Comentariensem . Numerarios . Adiutorem .
Aba¢tis . A libellis . Exceptores & c¢teros
officiales

osservare la sottoscritta norma
&
Primieramente imparerai di fare
questi dui tratti, cioe
dali qualise principiano tutte
le littere Cancellaresche,
Deli quali dui tratti l'uno é piano et
grosso, l'altro é acuto et sotti
le come qui tu puoi vedere
notato

While the basic shapes of our letters haven't changed much in hundreds of years, there have been thousands of variations on the theme. People have designed alphabets from human figures, architectural elements, flowers, trees, tools, and all sorts of everyday items, to be used as initials or typographic ornaments. Typefaces for reading, however,

Top inset: Italian manuscript, ca. 1530, shows how people wrote them. Bottom inset: From a book of writing instructions by Ludovico degli Arrighi, printed from engraved woodblocks, ca. 1521. The type on the page is Adobe Caslon Italic, designed by Carol Twombly in 1990. It is based on a British typeface from 200 years later, but still is remarkably similar to the Italian origin.

are generally derived from handwriting. Gutenberg's types followed the forms of the letters written by professional scribes in fifteenth-century Germany. The printers in Venice, a few decades later, also based their first types on local handwriting. Over the centuries, cultural differences have been expressed in the way people write. Professional scribes in European courts developed elaborate formal scripts. As literacy spread, people began to care more about expressing their thoughts quickly, and less about style and legibility.

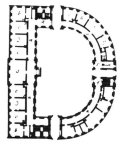

Quills, fountain pens, pencils, and felt-tip pens have all done their part to change the look of handwriting. The common denominator, the Roman alphabet, survived all these developments remarkably intact.

By the same token what was thought to be a fashionable house hundreds of years ago is still a very desirable house today. Fashion has changed remarkably since the 1400s, but people still wear shirts, trousers, socks, and shoes. The process of manufacturing them has changed, but materials such as wool, silk, and leather are still being used, and are often more desirable than their modern alternatives.

After all, the shape of the human body hasn't changed in the last 500 years, nor has the basic way we look at the world around us. Our view of things is still largely shaped by nature – plants, animals, weather, scenery. Most of what we perceive as harmonious and pleasing to the eye follows rules of proportion that are derived from nature. Our classic typefaces also conform to those rules; if they don't, we regard them as strange, at the least fashionable, and at the worst illegible.

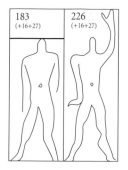

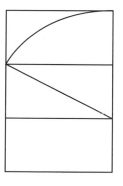

The human body hasn't changed drastically for centuries, so neither have things like shoes, fashion influences notwithstanding. Here is a collection of some footwear from the fifteenth century until today.

Some people have measured the human body to find what makes certain proportions look more beautiful than others.

Le Corbusier's Modulor (the system framing his ideas of modern functional architecture) is neatly related to a man with an outstretched arm. Not surprisingly (to anyone who's ever looked into the laws of harmonious proportions), the French architect found that the Golden Section was the underlying principle for all the measurements used in his drawings of the human body.

The first generation to grow up with
television (those born in the 1950s) is still
imitating and idolizing the lifestyles depicted
on TV. This generation is followed by one
growing up with music videos, multimedia,
and virtual reality. The manipulation of
sounds and images, the invention of artificial
realities, and life inside man-made surroundings puts to question our "natural"
rules of perception. And, as with every tech-
nological and cultural development in the last
2000 years, type and typography reflect this.
If current trends are anything to go by, the
look of typefaces is bound to change more by
the year 2000 than it has in all the years since
the fifteenth century. The next generation of
readers might consider things acceptable and,
indeed, highly legible, that we would today
consider ridiculous.

"It'll never catch on." Isn't that what people
said about almost every major discovery or
invention?

The first examples of a new
technology rarely resemble
their modern counterparts,
at least not in appearance.
If you look at the underlying
principles, however, they
were there already. If they
hadn't been, planes wouldn't
fly, TV tubes would explode,
and cars wouldn't be faster
than horse-drawn carriages.

Some new type designs
will not be around in
a few years. Others,
though they might look
strange today, could
herald the shape of
things to come.

From top to bottom:
F Moonbase Alpha by
Cornel Windlin, 1991.

F Decoder by
Gerard Unger, 1991.

FF Beowolf Serif 23
by Just van Rossum and
Erik van Blokland, 1990 –
a "random" font that
changes its appearence
everytime it's printed.

ABCDEFGHIJKLMNOPQRS
TUVWXYZabcdefghijklm
nopqrstuvwxyz

(dr·//9

DECODER

ABCDEFGHIJKLMNOP
QRSTUVWXYZabcdef
ghijklmnopqrstuvwxyz

Sometimes a cigar is just a cigar.

Sigmund Freud (1856–1939), known as the father of psycho-analysis, was an Austrian neurologist who developed techniques of free association of ideas and theorized that dreams are representative of repressed sexual desires. Things said without any forethought sometimes result in what is known as a Freudian slip.

CHAPTER 3

Looking at type

HEAD

have to be big and at the top

Display *type is meant to show off the advantages* **of the product inside the package it is printed on.**

Type in books hasn't changed much over the last five hundred years. Then again, the process of reading hasn't changed that much either. We might have electric lights, reading glasses, and more comfortable chairs, but we still need a quiet corner, a little time on our hands, and a good story. Paperbacks crammed full of poorly spaced type with narrow page margins are a fairly new invention, born out of economic necessities, i.e., the need to make a profit. Chances are the more you pay for a book, the closer it will look like a good historical model that dates back to the Renaissance. By the time we are adults, we have read so much that is set in what is considered "classic" typefaces that we all think Baskerville, Garamond, and Caslon are the most legible typefaces ever designed…

Newspaper typography has created some of the very worst typefaces, typesetting, and page layouts known to mankind. Yet we put up with bad line breaks, huge word spaces, and ugly type, because that is what we are used to. After all, who keeps a newspaper longer than it takes to read it? And if it looked any better, would we still trust it to be objective?

Small print is called small print even though it is actually only the type that is small. To overcome the physical limitations of letters being too small to be distinguishable, designers have gone to all sorts of extremes, making parts of letters larger and/or smaller, altering the space in and around them so ink doesn't blacken the insides of letters and obscure their shapes, or accentuating particular characteristics of individual letters. Another trick is to keep the letters fairly large, while at the same time making them narrower than is good for them or us so more of them will fit into the available space. Often enough, however, type is kept small deliberately, so that we have a hard time reading it – for example, insurance claims and legal contracts.

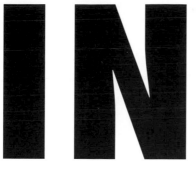

Anyone looking at a printed message will be influenced, within a split second of making eye contact, by everything on the page: the arrangement of various elements as well as the individual look of each one. In other words, an overall impression is created in our minds before we even start reading the first word. It's similar to the way we respond to a person's presence before we know anything about him or her, and then later find it difficult to revise our first impression.

We read best what we read most, even if it is badly set, badly designed, and badly printed. This is not to suggest there is a substitute for good type, great design, or clean printing, but a reminder of the fact that certain images are deeply ingrained in the reader's mind. Graphic designers, typesetters, editors, printers, and other communicators are well advised to be aware of these expectations. Sometimes it may be best to go by the rules; at other times the rules need to be broken to get the point across. Good designers learn all the rules before they start breaking them.

. **Handgloves**
FUTURA EXTRA BOLD COND.

. **Handgloves**
ANTIQUE OLIVE BLACK

. **Handglo**
BLACKOAK

. **Handgloves**
HOBO

. Handgloves
ADOBE CASLON REGULAR

. Handgloves
CANDIDA

. Handgloves
HELVETICA

Designing typefaces for particular purposes is more widespread than most people think. There are special types for telephone books, small ads, newspapers, and bibles, and for the exclusive use of corporations. There are also typefaces designed specially to comply with technical constraints, i.e., low-resolution printers, screen displays, monospaced typewriters, and optical character recognition. So far, all these typefaces have tried to emulate historical models. If there is a new alphabet coming up for the Millennium, it hasn't shown its face yet, not even on page 33. Below are types that have been designed for special purposes.

Bell Centennial
designed for telephone books.

ITC Weidemann
originally designed for a new edition of the bible.

Spartan Classified
made especially for small ads in newspapers.

VAG Rounded
Volkswagen's corporate typeface.

Sassoon Primary
for teaching handwriting to schoolchildren.

1

2

3

4

5

6

a Cooper Black	**b** MESQUITE
c Arnold Böcklin	**d** Berthold City
e Tekton	**f** Snell Roundhand

This is a typographic puzzle. Which typeface do you think fits which shoe? The answers are on the next page, but don't look now – that would be cheating. Remember which letter from the boxes on this page goes with which number from the opposite page, then turn the page and check against our personal favorites.

In some cases it is very easy to spot a typographic mistake.

39

1d Berthold City

2b MESQUITE

3f Snell Roundhand

4a Cooper Black

5c Arnold Böcklin

6e Tekton

No one would wear the same shoes to go dancing, run a mile, climb the northface of the Eiger, and walk to the office – not many people anyway. While your feet don't change shape, they need different sorts of support, protection or, indeed, enhancement to perform all the above tasks and many more besides.

This also applies to type. Sometimes the letters have to work hard to get across straight facts or numbers, or they may need to dress up the words a little to make them seem more pleasant, more comfortable, or simply prettier.

Some shoes fit your feet better than others, and you get to like them so much that you just want to keep buying the same kind over and over. Your friends, however, might begin to give you a rough time over your repetitious footwear, so why not buy a few pairs of the same models, but in different colors? Now you have more choices at the same comfort level.

As this page is only printed in two colors, we can't demonstrate the effect, but you can probably imagine it without too much visual prompting. Where's the analogy with type? Well, you can print it in different colors on different backgrounds, dark on light or light on dark. It will always look like you are actually using more than one typeface.

Your personal choice of typefaces to match the shoes will probably be quite different from the ones shown here. With more fonts to choose from than there are shoes in your typical shoe store, the task is daunting.

Luckily, the intended typographic purpose narrows the choice as much as the use you want to put your shoes to. Fortunately for the fashion-conscious designer, there are many options to choose from, even for similar design applications.

Cooper Black – see opposite page – is a very popular typeface, and was even more so twenty-five years ago. It has its advantages: nice and cuddly, heavy, and pretty unusual. But if you think it's been used a little too often, you can try Goudy Heavyface, ITC Souvenir Bold, Stemple Schneidler Black, or ITC Cheltenham Ultra. Compare them to each other and you will see they're all quite different, but might do the same job just as effectively.

Not all of us want to be seen wearing the same shoes as everybody else.

.**Handgloves**

GOUDY HEAVYFACE

.**Handgloves**

ITC SOUVENIR BOLD

.**Handgloves**

STEMPEL SCHNEIDLER BLACK

.**Handgloves**

ITC CHELTENHAM ULTRA

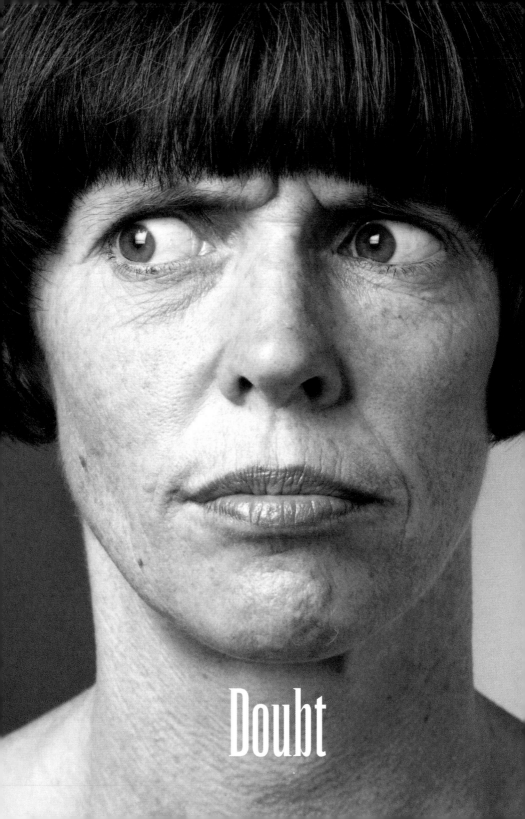

Doubt

So type has its practical uses – it can walk, run, skip, jump, climb, and dance. Can it also express emotions? Of course. If you look closely at a letter, you can see personality expressed in its physical characteristics: light or heavy, round or square, slim or squat. Letters can stand at attention next to each other like soldiers or they can dance gracefully on the line. Just as some words sound better than others, some words look nicer than others. That may be because we don't like the meaning of the word, but often we've formed an opinion before we've even read it. Isn't it nice that the *o* imitates the way we make our lips round to pronounce it? And how could the *i* stand for anything but the pointed sound it has in "pick"?

Dark emotions call for a black typeface with sharp edges; pleasant feelings are best evoked by informal, light characters. Or are they? The trouble is that as soon as you select a typeface that looks appropriate, put it on a page, surround it by space and perhaps other elements, it can take on a totally different look. So for the moment, we'll stick to choosing appropriate typefaces.

Runic Condensed is slightly awkward and definitely not suited for long passages. Its spiky serifs and exaggerated letterforms do not agree with classic theories of beauty and fine proportion. If unusual letterforms express uneasy feelings, these other condensed types might be a good choice. The last one might be suitable, not because it is condensed, but because it has slightly strange shapes.

Doubt?
Runic Condensed

Doubt?
Rockwell Condensed

Doubt?
Block Extra Condensed

Doubt?
Linoscript

Runic Condensed is a typeface from Monotype. Released in 1935, it replicates a late nineteenth-century display type.

Rockwell is perhaps the most popular slab-serif face. It was designed and produced by the Monotype Corporation in England under the direction of Frank Hinman Pierpont and first appeared in 1933. Rockwell was developed to answer a demand created by typefaces such as Memphis, Stymie, and Welt, which were released a few years earlier. Rockwell ended up overtaking them all in popularity.

Block is a family of typefaces originally designed by H. Hoffmann in 1908, with many subsequent versions released through 1926. Block simplified the setting of justified display lines with a system of capital and lowercase letters of varying widths that allowed the compositor to use the more extended alternate characters to fill out short lines. Block was the staple jobbing font for German printers well into the 1960s, when phototypesetting replaced hot metal. The irregular "mealy" outlines appeal to a modern audience, who like that recycled, used-before look.

Linoscript is a Morris Fuller Benton design released in 1905 as Typo Upright by American Type Founders; the design was later purchased by the Linotype Corporation for integration into their technology, which explains the current name.

43

Surprise

Some words are much more fun to find an appropriate typographic equivalent for than others. (Surprise, surprise.) It may be fairly difficult to find a majority agreement on the right typeface to spell "doubt," but this one shouldn't cause any problems.

What's more unexpected, more surprising then someone's handwriting? The best casual typefaces have always managed to carry some of the spontaneity of handwritten letters into the mechanical restrictions of typesetting. Even the names of some typefaces make you want to choose them. How about this one: Mistral – a cool wind blowing from the north into southern France. And indeed, in the south of France it seems to have become the standard typeface for every shopfront and delivery van.

In case you don't agree that Mistral suggests surprise, here are two alternatives.

Mistral was designed by Roger Excoffon in 1955. His other typefaces – Antique Olive, Choc, Banco – also show that typical Gallic style and have been enormously successful in France and other European countries.

Neville Brody, one of England's most influential graphic designers of the last decade or so, designed Arcadia in 1990. It was originally a headline font for the magazine *The Face*. In spite of its geometric origins, it looks surprisingly friendly and unexpected.

Auriol was designed by Georges Auriol in 1901. It combines floral ornaments with Japanese brushstrokes .

The complete freedom offered by computer applications makes type even more flexible – if a word doesn't look right when first set, you can manipulate the outlines until it does exactly what you want.

"Surprise" looks like it does on the right when it is set the way it comes out of the box. We didn't like the join between S and u, so we created outlines in Adobe Illustrator, cleaned up that detail (and a few others), and placed it in our photograph, where you can see the revised word. Most people would believe that it had been written by someone with a felt-tip pen, not simply set as part of a complete page. The other choices don't look quite so spontaneous, but surprising enough.

Mistral

Arcadia

Surprise

Auriol

JOY

The more characters in a word, the more chances there are to find the right letterforms to express its meaning. This word doesn't give us a lot of choices, just three characters: *j o y* or *J O Y*. Seeing that the lowercase *j* and *y* look so similar, an all-capital setting will work better with this one. All three typefaces here have a generous feel to them – open forms with confident strokes and a sense of movement.

ITC Kabel, Syntax, and Lithos are modern interpretations of classical letterforms; they maintain a chiseled look without formal stroke endings, which are known as *serifs*.

The letter *Y*, a latecomer to the Latin alphabet, is called *i grec* in French (Greek *i*). Its shape is derived from one of the calligraphic variations of the Greek upsilon.

It is nice to see that some words carry their own explanation in the letters. These free and easy shapes certainly make you think of a joyful person with arms in the air.

The original Kabel, designed by Rudolf Koch in 1927, has distinct Art Deco overtones, whereas International Typeface Corporation's 1976 version has a very generous x-height and is more regular and less quirky.

ITC Kabel Book

Syntax has the proportions of ancient Roman letters, but no serifs, making it both contemporary and classic looking. It was designed by Hans-Eduard Meier in 1968.

Syntax

Lithos is Carol Twombly's 1989 rendering of Greek inscriptions – just as elegant as Roman capitals, but less restrained. This face became an instant success and graphic designers use it for all sorts of trendy purposes, including titles for MTV, which goes to show that a classic can also be cheerful and modern.

JOY

Lithos Regular

.Handgloves

ITC KABEL BOOK

.Handgloves

SYNTAX

.HANDGLOVES

LITHOS REGULAR

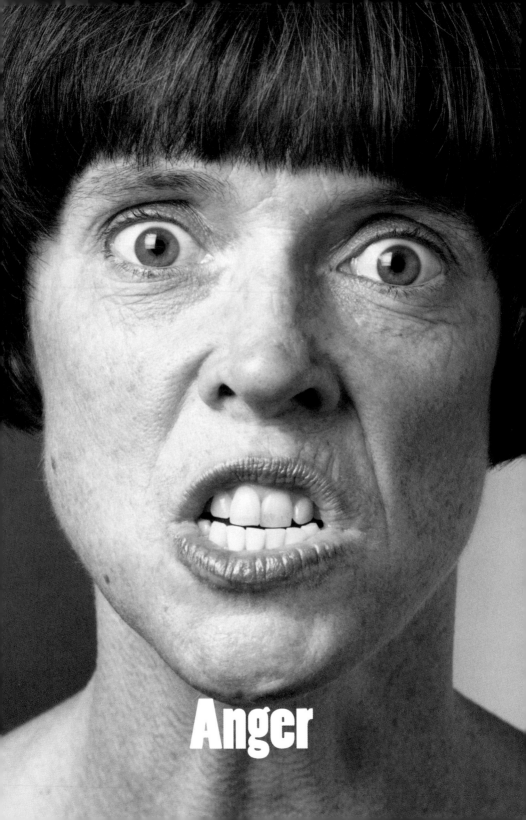

Anger

Anger, like doubt, can be described as a dark feeling that calls for a black, heavy typeface. Anger is not as narrow as doubt. It needs room to expand, sometimes to shout out loud.

It helps if the letters are not perfectly worked out and closed in on themselves, but rather a little irregular, leaving room for our imagination. A well-balanced Univers or Helvetica would not do.

Most really black typefaces have been overused because there aren't enough choices for the designers of posters and tabloid newspapers. These kinds of faces can be set with hardly any space between letters, which makes a large impact in a small space.

Futura Extrabold and ITC Franklin Gothic Heavy have been favorites for a long time, with Akzidenz Grotesk Super joining the Sumo-style fonts after it became available in the Adobe type library in 1992. All the way from the 1960s, Antique Olive Nord is making a comeback!

Flyer Extra Black Condensed, designed in 1962 by Konrad Bauer and Walter Baum.

Anger!

Flyer Extra Black Condensed

Poplar is a 1990 revival from Adobe of an old wood type from the mid-nineteenth century.

Anger!

Poplar

Block Heavy is the fattest member of the family. Its outlines are deliberately irregular, which helped prevent damage when metal type was printed on heavy platen presses. You could call it a pre-stressed design.

Anger!

Block Heavy

. **Handgloves**

FLYER EXTRA BLACK CONDENSED

. **Handgloves**

POPLAR

. **Handgloves**

BLOCK HEAVY

. **Handgloves**

FUTURA EXTRA BOLD

. **Handgloves**

ITC FRANKLIN GOTHIC HEAVY

. **Handgloves**

AKZIDENZ GROTESK SUPER

. **Handglove**

ANTIQUE OLIVE NORD

Handgloves

ITC Stone Serif

Handgloves

Imago Book

Handgloves

Freestyle Script

HANDGLOVES

Ironwood

Carta

There are seven deadly sins, seven seas, and seventh sons of seventh sons, but thousands of typefaces. Someone had to come up with a system to classify them, since describing how different type designs express different emotions just isn't exact enough. Unfortunately, there is not just one system, but quite a few, all of them too

The unofficial type classification – do not confuse with the official one on this page.

involved for anyone but the most devoted typomaniac. So here's the most rudimentary of ways to classify type. It's not historically correct, nor does it give a complete overview of the available choice of fonts. It simply shows that with just a few basic principles, hundreds of ways of designing typefaces become possible, the same way a few basic emotions evoke a million ways to make a face.

In case anyone wants it on record: here's the official Adobe type classification. We have chosen a typical typeface for each category, trying to avoid all the best-known ones.

VENETIAN

Handgloves

Centaur

GARALDE

Handgloves

Sabon

TRANSITIONAL

Handgloves

Janson Text

DIDONE

Handgloves

Bodoni Old Face

SLAB SERIF

Handgloves

Memphis

SANS SERIF

Handgloves

Syntax

GLYPHIC

Handgloves

Friz Quadrata

SCRIPT

Handgloves

Poetica

DISPLAY

Handgloves

Block

BLACKLETTER

Handgloves

Wilhelm Klingspor Gotisch

SYMBOLS

Universal News and Commercial Pi

Scientists have not been content with just calling the human face "beautiful" if it meets certain ideals, or "ugly" if it doesn't. They had to go out and measure proportions of nose to jaw, forehead to chin, and so on, to establish why some faces are more appealing than others.

Typographers and graphic designers often choose typefaces for the very same reason they might fancy a person: they just like that person. For more scientifically minded people, however, there are specific measurements, components, details, and proportions describing various parts of a letter. While these won't tell you what makes a typeface good, they will at least give you the right words to use when you discuss the benefits of a particular face over another. You can say "I hate the x-height on Such-a-Gothic" or "These descenders just don't work for me" or "Please, may I see something with a smaller cap height?" and you'll know what you're talking about.

Leonardo da Vinci tried to figure out what makes the human face look beautiful by measuring the proportions of the parts.

The problem with all these measurements is that there aren't any real standards for type designers to follow. Typographic features like large x-heights, wide counters, and exaggerated ascenders are no less slaves to fashion than the perpetual changes in skirt lengths dictated by what's shown on Paris runways.

The size of type, indicated in points (a point is .01384 inch; 12 points = 1 pica; 6 picas = 1 inch), is only a reminder of a historical convention, when type was cast on a body of metal. The body size of all 12-point type would have been the same, but the actual image on that body could be vastly different. Have a look at the 20-point types below – they don't have very much in common apart from the baseline.

The moral?
What you see is what you get – trust your eyes, not the scientific measurements.

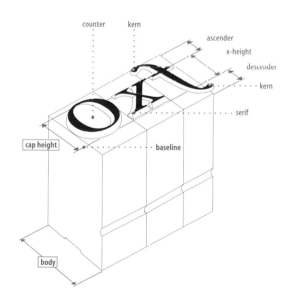

Sizes **Sizes** Sizes **Sizes** Sizes

The best part about playing the piano is that you don't have to lug around a saxophone.

Gerry Mulligan (1927–), master of the baritone saxophone, is one of the most versatile figures of modern jazz. He wrote his first arrangements and jazz compositions when he was still in his teens, and was part of the cool jazz scene in the 1940s; especially noteworthy were his pianoless groups in which his intricate and carefully balanced composing and arranging brought improvisation to new heights. He occasionally plays the piano.

CHAPTER 4

Type with a purpose

You know what it's like. It's late at night, your plane leaves at 6 a.m., you're still packing, and you just can't decide what to put into that suitcase.

Picking typefaces for a design job is a very similar experience. There are certain typefaces you are familiar with. You know how they will behave under certain circumstances, and you know where they are. On the other hand, there are those fashionable fonts that you've always wanted to use, but you're not quite sure if this job is the right one to experiment on. This is just like choosing which shoes to take on your trip – the comfortable ones are not the height of fashion, but the fashionable ones hurt. You might be able to stand them for a short reception, but not for shopping, let alone for a hike into the countryside.

Before you pack your font suitcase, you need to look at the task ahead. Strike a balance between practicalities and aesthetics – that's what design is all about.

While nobody has ever classified typefaces according to their problem-solving capabilities, many typefaces we use today were originally designed for particular purposes. Some of them are mentioned on page 37, but there are many more. Times New Roman was specially produced in 1931 for the London newspaper that gave its name to the typeface. In the late 1930s Mergenthaler Linotype in the USA (led by Chauncey H. Griffith) developed a group of five typefaces that were designed to be legible despite the rigors of newspaper printing. They were, not surprisingly, called the "Legibility Group," and a couple of them are still very popular today: Corona and Excelsior.

It might seem odd that legibility has to be made a special concern when designing a typeface, but there are plenty of fonts around that are meant to be seen, not read; it's very much like clothes that look great but barely protect the wearer from the elements.

.Handgloves

Times New Roman

.Handgloves

Corona

.Handgloves

Excelsior

Going on vacation doesn't necessarily mean traveling to a warm climate, but it always means we can leave behind many of our conventions, including the way we normally dress – or have to dress, as the case may be. You pick your clothes according to what is practical: easy to pack, easy to clean, and according to what is fun: casual, colorful, loose, and maybe a little more daring than what you would wear in your hometown.

The typographic equivalents are those typefaces that are comfortable to read, but which may be a little more idiosyncratic than your run-of-the-mill stuff. Serifs, too, can be casual, and "loose fit" is actually a typesetting term describing letters that have a comfortable amount of space between them.

As it happens, quite a few of the very early typefaces from the Renaissance and their modern equivalents fit that description. They still show their kinship with Italian handwriting, which by necessity had to be more casual than rigid metal letters. If you were a scribe in the papal office and had to write hundreds of pages every day, you wouldn't be able to take the time to fuss over formal capitals. So the scribes developed a fluent, cursive handwriting, which today we call italic, because it was invented in Italy.

You will have noticed that this whole page is set in a cursive font, and it feels quite comfortable. The rule says that you can't set whole pages, let alone books, in the italics of a typeface. The only reason it might not work is because we're not used to it. As pointed out on page 37, we read best what we read most. But that's no reason not to take a vacation from our daily habits and look at something different, at least once a year.

Some typefaces have a leisurely look about them while conforming to everyday typographic expectations. Others were born with unusual, yet casual, shapes and make the best of it.

Stempel Schneidler combines friendly letter shapes and high legibility – you can use it every day without it becoming restrictive like a necktie.

A recent typeface that looks casual, even "nice" but is still good for real work is ITC Flora. It was designed by the Dutch type designer Gerard Unger in 1980 and named after his daughter. Ellington, released in 1990, is a new design by Michael Harvey, the English lettering artist and stone carver. Both typefaces are quite unusual and therefore, not often thought of as useful text faces. But they are.

Many typefaces designed to look "friendly" tend to be patronizing. They can be so nice that you quickly get tired of them. When you're looking for casual typefaces, the obvious candidates are, of course, all of the scripts. Most, however, are not suited to long spells of reading, just as sandals are very comfortable, but not for walking on rocky roads.

.Handgloves

STEMPEL SCHNEIDLER

.Handgloves

ITC FLORA

.Handgloves

ELLINGTON

Most type is used for business communication of one sort or another, so it has to conform with written and unwritten rules of the corporate world. Just as business types are expected to wear a suit (plus, naturally a shirt and tie underneath), text set for business has to look fairly serious and go about its purpose in an inconspicuous, well-organized way. Typefaces like Times New Roman and Helvetica fit that bill perfectly, not for their particular suitability but more for their lack of individualism.

However, because it is now permissible in traditional business circles to wear fashionable ties and even venture into the realm of Italian suits that are not black or dark blue, typographic taste in those circles has widened to include other typefaces, from Palatino to Frutiger.

Generally, it is very simple to tell a particular business by the typefaces it prefers: the more technical the profession, the cooler and more rigidly constructed the typefaces have to be (Univers for architects); the more traditional the trade, the more classical they are (Bodoni for bankers).

The trouble is, there is no law against speculators using a real classic, trustworthy typeface for their brochures, lending these unsavory individuals typographic credibility, if nothing else.

To show the subtle differences between fonts at this size, we've set the copy on the left in a variety of faces, one for each paragraph. Handgloves at the bottom of this column show them one after the other.

Frutiger, originally designed in 1976 by Adrian Frutiger for the signage at the Charles de Gaulle airport in Paris, has recently become one of the more popular typefaces for corporate use.

Palatino, designed by Hermann Zapf in 1952, owes its popularity – especially in the USA – largely to its availability as a core font on PostScript laserprinters. It is nevertheless a welcome alternative to other less suitable serif fonts.

Adrian Frutiger designed Univers in 1957. It was the first typeface to be planned with a coordinated range of weights and widths, comprising twenty-one related designs.

Bodoni Old Face is one of many redesigns of Giambattista Bodoni's classic typefaces from the late eighteenth century. This one, by Günter Gerhard Lange shows more color and stroke variations than other Bodoni revivals.

.Handgloves

Frutiger

.Handgloves

Palatino

.Handgloves

Univers

.Handgloves

Bodoni Old Face

If it were just a little heavier, News Gothic by Morris Fuller Benton, 1908, would be a favorite workhorse typeface. But until the heavier version from Linotype is made available in digital form, ITC Franklin Gothic, also designed by Benton, in 1904, fits the bill almost as well. The new condensed versions will improve the usefulness of this family even further.

For a good range of weights, look at Avenir, Adrian Frutiger's 1988 interpretation of Futura. Lucida Sans, by Kris Holmes and Charles Bigelow, 1985, has sturdy, rugged letter shapes. Its sister typeface, Lucida, remains one of the best choices for business communication printed on laserprinters and fax machines.

The coordinated range of Sumner Stone's 1987 original design, ITC Stone Sans, Serif, and Informal, can also work hard. You should also look at the condensed weights of Frutiger. The real winner has to be this very face, Myriad, designed by Carol Twombly and Robert Slimbach in 1991. Multiple master technology allows you to create exactly the weight and width needed for the particular requirements, both aesthetically and technically. Myriad is neutral enough to stay in the background, but has that little extra personality to shine when necessary.

■ Calling a typeface a "real workhorse" doesn't mean that others don't work, it just means that there are some out there that don't look very glamorous and are consequently not often known by name; these types, however, are used every day by designers and typesetters because of their reliability.

▶ If you set a catalog for machine parts, or instructions on how to use a fire extinguisher, you're not worried about subtly curved serifs or classicist contrast. You need letters that are: clearly distinguishable; compact, so quite a few of them fit into a limited space (is there ever enough space?); and sturdy, so they can withstand the rigors of printing and copying.

Here's what is needed in a hardworking typeface:

1 A good regular weight – not so thin that it will disappear on a photocopy (everything gets copied more than once these days), and not so heavy that the letter shapes fill in.

2 At least one bold weight, with enough contrast to be noticed, to complement the regular weight.

3 Very legible numbers – they have to work particularly hard because confusing figures can be at the least annoying and at the worst downright dangerous.

4 Economy – it should be narrow enough to fit a lot of copy into the available space, but not actually compressed beyond recognition. A typeface fitting this description would also do very well on faxes.

Handgloves
Handgloves
News Gothic · News Gothic Bold

Handgloves
Handgloves
ITC Franklin Gothic · ITC Franklin Gothic Bold

Handgloves
Handgloves
Avenir · Avenir Heavy

Handgloves
Handgloves
Lucida Sans · Lucida Sans Bold

Handgloves
Handgloves
Lucida · Lucida Bold

Handgloves
Handgloves
ITC Stone Sans · ITC Stone Sans Bold

Handgloves
Handgloves
ITC Stone Serif · ITC Stone Serif Bold

Handgloves
Handgloves
ITC Stone Informal · ITC Stone Informal Bold

Handgloves
Handgloves
Frutiger Condensed · Frutiger Condensed Bold

Handgloves
Handgloves
Myriad Multiple Master

One

of the few sanctuaries for old aristocratic traditions is

Society.

Top hats, cummerbunds, patent leather shoes, and coats with tails are all remnants of the eighteenth century, when countries were run by kings and queens who spoke French to each other and their entourages.

Snell Roundhand

Not

much of that remains, except for maîtres d'hôtel at posh restaurants who fake French accents and wear coats with tails.

❖

Künstler Script

Of course,

French is still the official language of the diplomatic corps Typographically speaking, we have reminders of these somewhat feudal traditions in the accepted and expected ways of designing invitations and programs.

✳

Snell Roundhand

CENTERED TYPE AND
A PREFERENCE FOR FONTS THAT COME
FROM A GOOD BACKGROUND IN
COPPER ENGRAVING OR
UPPER CRUST CALLIGRAPHY.

AND, OF COURSE,
THOSE VERY FAMILIAR FOUR LETTERS "R S V P"
WHICH MEAN
"PLEASE LET US KNOW WHETHER YOU'RE GOING TO BE THERE."
BUT ACTUALLY STANDS FOR
"RÉPONDEZ S'IL VOUS PLAÎT."

Copperplate Gothic

There is no category known as "formal fonts," but a number of typefaces come from that background. The text on the left is set in Snell Roundhand, a formal script from the 1700s, redesigned in 1965 by Matthew Carter.

Apart from formal scripts such as Snell, Künstler Script, and others like it, there are the aptly named copperplates. They look formal and distinguished and are even available in a range of weights and versions, but they all lack one important feature: lowercase characters.

Other typefaces that owe their appearance to the process of engraving into steel as opposed to writing with a quill or cutting into wood are Berthold Walbaum, Bauer Bodoni, or ITC Fenice. They can look formal and aristocratic enough to make a favorable impression when printed on expensive paper.

O N THE TOWN

Akzidenz Grotesk Super

Cochin

Going out on the town allows us to do the things we don't get to do in the office, and we get to wear all the trendy stuff that we can never resist buying but don't seem to really need on a day-to-day basis.

What makes typefaces trendy is almost unpredictable – much to the chagrin of the people who have to market them. Sometimes it takes just one highly visible project, such as MTV's use of Lithos, and sometimes the designer is at the right place with the right type.

trendy types

DIN Mittelschrift

There are typefaces that are only suitable for the more o c c a s i o n a l o c c a s i o n. They might be too hip to be used for mainstream communication, or they could simply be to uncomfortable – a bit like wearing very tight jeans rather than admit they don't fit us any longer. Very often these off-beat fonts are both – tight in the crotch and extrovert.

The trouble is that it still takes a couple of years for a typeface to get from idea to release, often longer.

Right now – the end of 1992 – people have started discovering Akzidenz Grotesk Super, because everybody needs a very heavy sans serif; DIN Mittelschrift, commonly known as DIN-Schrift, seems to back the trend for non-design, as do OCR B, and old typewriter faces. Cochin Italic has been in demand for a while, presumably for its off-beat, slightly old-fashioned appearance. Lithos is everywhere, although the designer never dreamed that anybody would use this re-creation of ancient Greek inscriptions for electronic entertainment. Neville Brody's Industria and Insignia reflect the 1980s.

Lithos

FUN FONTs

Cochin italic

The entertainment value of this sort of typographical work is often higher than that of the straightforward corporate stuff, so there's a great deal of satisfaction from not only the words, but also from the fun of being able to work with really unusual fonts.

Industria

Fashionable faces

Insignia

One thing leather jackets have on trendy typefaces is that the jackets get better as they get older, which is more than can be said about some of the faces we loved in the 1970s but would be too embarrassed to ask for now. Like all fashions, however, they keep coming back. Don't throw away your old fonts - keep them for your kids.

No, Watson, this was not done by accident, but by design.

Sherlock Holmes is a fictional detective created by Sir Arthur Conan Doyle (1859–1930). Holmes' extraordinary powers of deductive reasoning carry him, along with his somewhat befuddled partner Dr. Watson, through some of the most complex mysteries in detective fiction.

CHAPTER 5

Type builds character

The Way to Wealth

BENJAMIN FRANKLIN

If time is of all things the most precious, wasting time must be the greatest prodigality; since lost time is never found again, and what we call time enough always proves too little. Let us then be up and doing, and doing to a purpose, so by diligence we should do more with less perplexity. Sloth makes all things difficult, but industry all things easy. He that riseth late must trot all day and shall scarce overtake the business at night; while laziness travels so slowly that poverty soon overtakes him. Sloth, like rust, consumes faster than labor wears, while the used key is always bright. Do not squander time, for that's the stuff life is made of; how much more than is necessary do we spend in sleep, forgetting that the sleeping fox catches no poultry, and that there will be sleeping enough in the grave.

So what signifies wishing and hoping for better times? We may make these times better if we bestir ourselves. Industry need not wish, and he that lives upon hope will die fasting. There are no gains without pains and he that has a trade has an estate, and he that has a calling has an office of profit and honor. But then the trade must be worked at and the calling well followed. Though you have found no treasure, nor has any rich relation left you a legacy, diligence is the mother of good luck, and all things are given to industry. Plow deep while sluggards sleep, and you will have corn to sell and keep; work while it is called today or you know not how much you may be hindered tomorrow: one today is worth two tomorrows, and farther: have you something to do tomorrow, do it today.

Be ashamed to catch yourself idle. When you have so much to do, be up by the peep of day. Let not the sun look down and say: "Inglorious here he lays." Handle your tools without mittens; remember, that the cat in gloves catches no mice. It is true there is much to be done, and perhaps you are weak-handed, but stick to it steadily, and you will see great

The way we read books hasn't changed very much over the last 500 years, so the way books look hasn't had to change either. Only the economics have changed, which means that publishers today insist on fitting more type onto a page, and they aren't always prepared to pay for good typesetting, let alone for someone to actually design the inside of a book, not just the cover. Every dollar spent on printing a book puts seven dollars or more on its price in the bookstore.

The lefthand pages in this chapter have been reduced to fit into this book; most are about two-thirds their actual size.

Cheap paperbacks, therefore, do not usually represent the state of the art, typographically speaking. Generally they could be nicer than they are because it costs the same to observe the basic rules of book layout using a good, legible typeface as it does to ignore the rules and set it in whatever the printer happens to have around.

To show just how much type can accomplish and how versatile it is, we have used the same text, written by Benjamin Franklin in 1733, to set all the samples in this chapter; a few liberties have been taken with Mr. Franklin's words to make typographic points.

Our example is set in Adobe Caslon, Carol Twombly's 1990 version of one of the most popular of all the book faces (originally designed by William Caslon in 1725); we also use the Adobe Caslon Expert set (see page 99). The Irish playwright George Bernard Shaw insisted that all his books be set in Caslon, earning him the title "Caslon man at any rate." For decades the motto of British printers was, "When in doubt, set it in Caslon."

The layout follows the classic model with wide margins, generous space between lines, and a centered title. To achieve a nice, smooth edge on both sides of the column, the punctuation is hung in the

.Handgloves
ADOBE CASLON

.HANDGLOVES
ADOBE CASLON EXPERT

ADOBE CASLON ORNAMENTS

Frugality will never go out of style.

To be secure, certainty and success rely on a dependable financial institution.

It's easy to think that a little tea or a little punch now and then, a diet a little more costly, clothes a little finer, and a little entertainment is no great matter. But at the Bank of Benjamin we think that being aware of small expenses is just as important as the consideration it takes, say, to purchase a home: small leaks will surely sink a great ship. Our financial advisors will always be available to advise the best ways to put your savings to work. We know that what often appears to be a terrific investment, quite frequently turns out otherwise. So when confronted by a great pennysworth, our advisors will pause a while: Cheapness is apparent only, and not real. We want our customers to enjoy their hard-earned leisure without having to think about their hard-earned dollars. So be sure to keep this in mind: if you won't listen to reason, it will rap your knuckles.

There also seems to be a generic style for advertisements. Although advertising does not have a lengthy tradition (it has only been around about a hundred years), its style is as established as the traditional book.

Headline on top, attention-grabbing picture underneath, subhead, main copy, logo, pay-off line, address or telephone number. Never more than eight elements! People are able to comprehend just about that many different pieces in one message; as soon as there are more, it requires too many takes, and attention goes elsewhere.

You can also recognize a serious, idea-based advertisement by the serious typography. No experiments here – take a classic, well-tried typeface, arrange it in a predictable layout and people might actually read the message.

When Paul Renner started work on Futura in 1924, it was proclaimed as the "typeface for our time," alluding to the social democratic reform of German society in the 1920s. The first weight was released in 1927.

. Handgloves
FUTURA BOOK

. Handgloves
FUTURA BOOK OBLIQUE

. Handgloves
FUTURA CONDENSED BOLD

. Handgloves
FUTURA CONDENSED BOLD OBLIQUE

. Handgloves
FUTURA HEAVY

. Handgloves
FUTURA HEAVY OBLIQUE

. Handgloves
FUTURA BOLD

. Handgloves
FUTURA BOLD OBLIQUE

. Handgloves
FUTURA EXTRA BOLD

. Handgloves
FUTURA CONDENSED EXTRA BOLD

. Handgloves
FUTURA COND. EXTRA BOLD OBLIQUE

. Handgloves
FUTURA EXTRA BOLD OBLIQUE

. Handgloves
FUTURA LIGHT

. Handgloves
FUTURA LIGHT OBLIQUE

. Handgloves
FUTURA CONDENSED LIGHT

. Handgloves
FUTURA CONDENSED LIGHT OBLIQUE

. Handgloves
FUTURA

. Handgloves
FUTURA CONDENSED

. Handgloves
FUTURA CONDENSED OBLIQUE

. Handgloves
FUTURA OBLIQUE

Time Line

A lecture by Frank Franklin

If time is the most precious of all things, wasting time must be the greatest sin. Lost time is never found again, and what we call enough time is never enough. Let us then be up and doing, and doing with a purpose, so by diligence we should do more with less perplexity. Sloth makes all things difficult, but industry all things easy. He that riseth late must trot all day and shall scarce overtake the business at night; while laziness travels so slowly that poverty soon overtakes him. Do not squander time, for that's the stuff life is made of; how much more than is necessary do we spend in sleep, forgetting that the sleeping fox catches no poultry, and that there will be sleeping enough in the grave.

7:00 p.m.
Saturday, December 12
Oakland Coliseum

You may think, perhaps, that a little tea, or a little punch now and then, diet a little more costly, clothes a little finer, and little entertainment now and then, can be no great matter. Watch those little expenses, a small leak will sink a great ship, and moreover, fools make feasts, and wise men eat them. Buy what you have no need for and before long you shall sell your necessities. Many a one, for the sake of finery on the back have gone with a hungry belly. Silks and satins, scarlet and velvets, put out the kitchen fire. By these and other extravagances the genteel are reduced to poverty.

He that riseth late must trot all day and shall scarce overtake the business at night

Remember this, however, if you won't be counseled, you can't be helped, and further: If you will not listen to reason, it will surely rap your knuckles.

If you will not listen | to reason, it will surely | rap your knuckles.

Among the many varieties of contemporary graphic design styles, "new wave" is just another tag describing a fresh approach to integrating images, type, and other elements on a page. This new-wave style makes ample use of the computer's vocabulary – deliberate bitmaps, gradations of color, overlaid images, frames, lines, boxes.

The choice of typefaces tends to give away one of the main influences for this, the American new wave: Swiss typography, the Basel school. Sans serif faces dominate and many of them happen to be of Swiss origin – Helvetica (as well as its German predecessor, Akzidenz Grotesk), Univers, Frutiger. Add a few trendy fonts from independent designers here and there and you have the right mix.

Luckily for professional designers, this sounds easier than it is. If everybody could be a successful designer by following simple recipes, we'd be out of work tomorrow. But that extra ingredient, a concept, an idea, cannot be formulated as easily as this. The waves may come and go, but graphic design will always be about problem solving first, and style making afterward.

For this exercise, we have not shown everything we could on a page. We haven't gone crazy with sampling images, overlaying them as if there were no tomorrow or using the weirdest fonts available.

Instead, we've picked the typeface that is gradually replacing Helvetica as Corporate World Font No. 1. Frutiger (see page 61) is now available in a good range of weights and widths, making it suitable for almost every typographic task. It avoids Helvetica's blandness, adding instead a more humanistic touch. This improves legibility by keeping letter shapes open and more distinct from one another.

The condensed weights are particularly suitable for projects that need a clean-looking, highly legible, fairly neutral, and space-saving typeface.

.Handgloves

Frutiger Light

.Handgloves

Frutiger Roman

.Handgloves

Frutiger Bold Condensed

.*Handgloves*

Frutiger Black Italic

Comparison of critical letter shapes in Akzidenz Grotesk, the mother of most modern sans serifs; Helvetica, the face without features; Univers, the cool alternative; and Frutiger, the friendly sans.

Industry need not wish, if you live on hope you will die fasting.
If you have a trade, you have an estate, and if you have a calling you have an office of profit and honor.

*I*f time is the most precious of all things, wasting time must be the greatest sin; since lost time is never found again, and what we call enough time always proves to be too little. Let's be up and doing, and with a purpose, so by diligence we can do more with less perplexity.

Sloth makes all things difficult, but industry all things easy. If you get up late you must trot all day and barely take overtake the business at night; while laziness travels so slowly that poverty will soon overtake you. Sloth, like rust, consumes faster than labor wears, while the used key is always bright. Time is the stuff life is made of; how much more than is necessary do we spend in sleep, forgetting that the sleeping fox catches no poultry, and that there will be sleeping enough in the grave.

Industry need not wish, if you live on hope you will die fasting. If you have a trade, you have an estate, and if you have a calling you have an office of profit and honor. But then the trade must be worked at and the calling well followed.

F. F. Franklin
First Corporate Officer

Though you have found no treasure, nor has any rich relation left you no legacy, diligence is the mother of good luck, and all things are given to industry. Plow deep while sluggards sleep, and you will have corn to sell and keep; work while it is called today or you know not how much you may hindered tomorrow: one today is worth two tomorrows, and furthermore: if you have something to do tomorrow, do it today. If you want a faithful servant, and one that you like, serve yourself. Be circumspect and caring, even in the smallest matters, because sometimes a little neglect breeds great mischief: for want of a nail the shoe was lost, for want of a shoe the horse was lost, being soon overtaken and stolen by the enemy.

Pension Assets Exceed $12 Billion

So much for industry, and attention to one's own business, but to these we must add frugality, if we would make our industry more successful. We think of saving as well as of getting. You may think, perhaps, that a little tea, or a little punch now and then, a diet that's a little more

Corporations spend a good deal of money to show their shareholders, their customers, and their banks how good they are (the corporations, not the others). So they hire designers or advertising agencies (there is a difference) to design brochures, booklets, and annual reports to make them look as good as they wished they were.

Strangely enough, as anyone who's ever been on a design jury judging annual reports or other corporate messages could testify, many of these printed pieces come out looking very similar. Although some designers set trends and others follow them, they all get paid to make their clients look different from the competition.

It is, therefore, easy enough to design a typically corporate page, at least for the USA. In Europe, this page would look quite different, but with definite similarities within certain countries. You can always tell a German report from a Dutch, British, or Italian one, but they all have one thing in common: the picture of the chairman.

Judging from the typeface used, the page on the left must be for a financial or similar institution. It is set in Bodoni, and the layout combines classic elements such as the centered sidebar with traditional advertising conventions, and justified text across a column that is far too narrow to achieve reasonable word breaks and word spaces (more about that in chapter 7).

While you can't go wrong with Bodoni, you could, however, try a different version now and again. Berthold, Linotype, and Monotype Bodonis are very much alike, whereas Bauer Bodoni has so much contrast between thick and thin lines that it isn't really suitable for small sizes. Bodoni Old Face is much better at small sizes than all the others. Its little quirks become visible only at large sizes, which might be desirable, as they will add a little life to your pages.

The Bodonis have grown into a large family – everybody who is anybody in the type world offers a different version. Here are a few of the styles and weights available.

.Handgloves
BERTHOLD BODONI LIGHT

.Handgloves
BODONI BOOK

.Handgloves
BERTHOLD BODONI REGULAR

.Handgloves
BERTHOLD BODONI OLD FACE

.Handgloves
BAUER BODONI BOLD

.Handgloves
BODONI

.Handgloves
BERTHOLD BODONI MEDIUM

.Handgloves
BERTHOLD BODONI OLD FACE MED.

.Handgloves
BAUER BODONI BOLD

.Handgloves
BODONI BOLD

.Handgloves
BERTHOLD BODONI BOLD

.Handgloves
BAUER BODONI BLACK

.Handgloves
BAUER BODONI BLACK CONDENSED.

.Handgloves
BODONI POSTER COMPRESSED

▶ *Time as a Tool.* **Benny Frank. Philadelphia: Caslon Publishing, 1992. 790pp. Hardcover. $19.95.**
From Time as a Tool: "If time is the most precious of all things, wasting time must be the greatest sin; since lost time is never found again, and what we call time enough always proves too little. Do not squander time, for that's the stuff life is made of; how much more than is necessary do we spend in sleep, forgetting that the sleeping fox catches no poultry, and that there will be sleeping enough in the grave."

▶ *Circumspection at Work.* **Fran Benjamin. Philadelphia: Caslon Publishing, 1991. 145pp. Softcover. $8.95.**
From Circumspection at Work: "So what signifies wishing and hoping for better times? We could make these times better if we bestir ourselves. Industry need not wish, and he that lives upon hope will die fasting. There are no gains without pains. If you have a trade you have an estate, and and if you have a calling you have an office of profit and honor. But then the trade must be worked at and the calling well followed. Though you have found no treasure, nor has any rich relation left you no legacy, diligence is the mother of good luck, and all things are given to industry. Plow deep while sluggards sleep, and you will have corn to sell and keep; work while it is called today or you know not how much you may hindered tomorrow: one today is worth two tomorrows, and farther: have you something to do tomorrow, do it today."

Sales Tax

We are required to collect sales tax on shipments to the states listed below. Please add the correct percentage amount. If you pay by credit card and don't know your sales tax, leave the line blank and we will fill in the correct amount.

▶ *Time & Saving.* **Jamie Franklin. Philadelphia: Caslon Publishing, 1991. Softcover. $8.95.**
From Time & Saving: "We must consider frugality, if we want to make our work more certainly successful. A person may, if she doesn't know how to save as she gets, keep her nose all her life to the grindstone, and die not worth a penny at the last. A fat kitchen does make a lean will. Think of saving as well as of getting. A small leak will sink a great ship, Cheapness is apparent only, and not real; the bargain, by straitening you in business, might do you more harm than good. 'At a great pennyworth, pause awhile'. "

Ordering Information

.... California
.... Connecticut
.... Florida
.... Georgia
.... Illinois
.... Massachusetts
.... Maryland
.... Missouri
.... Minnesota
.... New Jersey
.... New Mexico
.... New York
.... Ohio
.... Pennsylvania
.... Texas
.... Virginia
.... Washington

Name

Address

City   **State**   **Zip**   **Country**

Telephone   **Date of Purchase**

Book Title   **Quantity**

Book Title   **Quantity**

Book Title   **Quantity**

Subtotal

Sales Tax

Shipping (please add $2 per book)

Total Order

Method of Payment

.... **Check or money order enclosed, payable to TimeSaving Books Ltd.**

.... **Please charge my credit card**

Credit Card Number   **Expiration Date**

.... **Visa/MasterCard**   .... **American Express**

Signature (required for credit card purchases)

One of the areas typographers usually stay well clear of is the design of forms. They are not the easiest things to design, and in that respect should be considered a challenge. They offer enormous rewards – not winning awards or being included in the design annuals, but in terms of achievement.

Forms always have too much copy, so first choose a font that is narrower than your run-of-the-mill ones. Make sure it is clearly legible, has a good bold weight for emphasis, and has readable numbers.

Keep the preprinted information clearly separated from the areas you want people to fill in. These lines should be inviting guides for people's handwriting, and not look like bars on a prison cell window. The same goes for boxes around text. Who needs them? Some people seem to be afraid that the type might fall off the page if there isn't a box around it: it won't happen! Without restricting boxes, forms don't look half as forbidding and official. Different areas on the page can be separated by white space, as shown in our example.

If any typeface was designed to be neutral, clean, and practical, it is Univers, designed by Adrian Frutiger, 1957. The condensed versions of this typeface are actually quite legible, considering how much copy can fit into a confined space.

There are twenty-seven versions of Univers in the Adobe type library, from Univers 39 (ultra condensed thin) to Univers 83 (extra black extended). The numbering system is very simple. The first digit stands for the weight: 3 is very light, 9 is very heavy, so 5 is medium. A 5 in the second place means it's the roman version (i.e., upright), 6 for oblique, 7 for condensed, 8 for condensed oblique, 9 for extra condensed, 3 for extended, 4 for extended oblique. Easy, isn't it? So easy, in fact, that this system has been applied to a number of other large families of typefaces, for example, Neue Helvetica, Frutiger, Centennial, Glypha, and Serifa.

This table shows how all the weights of Univers relate to each other. The numbering system makes sense – once you've thought about it.

BY FRANK BENJAMIN

The Time Is
NOW!

I f time be of all things the most precious, wasting time must be the greatest prodigality; since lost time is never found again, and what we call time enough always proves little enough. Let us then be up and doing, and doing to a purpose, so by diligence we should do more with less perplexity. Sloth makes all things difficult, but industry all things easy. He that riseth late must trot all day and

shall scarce overtake the business at night, while soon overtakes him. Sloth, like rust, consumes faster than labor wears, while the used key is always bright. Do not squander time, for that's the stuff life is made of; how much more than is necessary do we spend in sleep, forgetting that the sleeping fox catches no poultry, and that there will be sleeping enough in the grave.

So what signifies wishing and hoping for better times? We may make these times better if we stir ourselves. Industry need not wish, and he that lives upon hope will die fasting. There are no gains without pains. If you have a trade you have an estate, and if you have a calling you have an office of profit and honor. But then the trade must be worked at and the calling well followed. Though you have found no treasure, nor has any rich relation left

> **"Wise men learn by others' harms, fools scarcely by their own"**

you no legacy, diligence is the mother of good luck, and all things are given to industry. Plow deep while sluggards sleep, and you will have corn to sell and keep; work while it is called today or you know not how much you may hindered tomorrow: one today is worth two tomorrows, and farther: have you something to do tomorrow, do it today. If you want a faithful servant, and one that you like, serve yourself. Be circumspect and caring, even in the smallest matters, because sometimes a little neglect breeds great mischief: for want of a nail the shoe was lost, for want of a shoe the horse was lost, being soon overtaken and stolen by the enemy, all for want of care of a horseshoe nail.

You may think, perhaps, that a little tea, or a little punch now and then, diet a little more costly, clothes a little finer, and little entertain-

Magazines are perhaps one of the best indicators of a country's current typographical taste; most of them get redesigned often enough to be on top of contemporary cultural inclinations. Magazine publishing is a very competitive business, and design plays a significant role in the way magazines present themselves to the general public.

Depending on the readership, magazines can look old-fashioned, conservative, pseudo-classic, trendy, cool, technical, newsy, and noisy. All these signals are conveyed by typography, which may or may not be an adequate representation of the editorial contents.

For our example, we have chosen the safe way – a traditional look. The page uses ITC Berkeley Oldstyle, one of the most American of typefaces, and employs all the paraphernalia of "good" editorial layout: drop capitals, letterspaced headlines, scotch rules, large pull-quotes, italic lead-ins, and a contrasting bold sans serif. This sort of layout is supposed to appeal to people between thirtysomething and the midlife crisis, who apparently are willing to read more than a couple of paragraphs in one sitting.

Similarities with existing publications may be spotted by colleagues from the trade – this is not necessarily unintentional.

ITC Berkeley Oldstyle is a new version of University of California Oldstyle, the typeface Frederic Goudy designed in 1938 for the University of California Press in, yes, Berkeley. It was brought out first as Californian in 1957, and in its current form by the International Typeface Corporation in 1983. It is, like most of Goudy's designs, quirky enough to make it interesting looking, but never silly.

ITC Berkeley Oldstyle's cheerful but restrained appearance makes it a good companion for bold sans serifs, particularly those with similar eccentricities like ITC Franklin Gothic. The original Franklin Gothic was designed a generation before University of California Oldstyle, in 1904, by Morris Fuller Benton.

.Handgloves

ITC BERKELEY OLDSTYLE BOOK

.Handgloves

ITC BERKELEY OLDSTYLE

.Handgloves

ITC BERKELEY OLDSTYLE BOLD

.Handgloves

ITC FRANKLIN GOTHIC CONDENSED

.Handgloves

ITC FRANKLIN GOTHIC EXTRA COND.

.Handgloves

ITC FRANKLIN GOTHIC NO. 2

Good Times, Better Times

"Inglorious here he lays."

Frances Franklin

Be ashamed to catch yourself idle. When you have so much to do, be up by the peep of day. Handle your tools without mittens; remember, that the cat in gloves catches no mice. There is much to be done, and perhaps you are weak-handed, but stick to it, and you will see great effects, for constant dropping wears away stones; and by diligence and patience, the mouse ate in two the cable, and allow me to add, little strokes fell great oaks. If you want a faithful servant, and one that you like, serve yourself. Be circumspect and caring, even in the smallest matters, because sometimes a little neglect breeds great mischief.For want of a nail the shoe was lost, for want of a shoe the horse was lost, being soon overtaken and stolen by the enemy, all for want of care of a horseshoe nail.

New! So much for industry, and attention to one's own business, but we must add frugality to these if we want to make our industry more successful. A person may, if she doesn't know how to save as she gets, keep her

Wishing and hoping for better times? We can make these times better if we bestir ourselves. Industry need not wish, and if you live upon hope you will die fasting. If you have a trade, you have an estate, and if you are lucky enough to have a calling, you have an office of profit and honor. But the trade must be worked at and the calling well followed. Though you have found no treasure, nor has any rich relation left you no legacy, remember that diligence is the mother of good luck, and all things are given to industry. Work while it is called today because you don't know how much you may hindered tomorrow: one today is worth two tomorrows, and don't forget: if you have something to do tomorrow, do it today.

Today's counterculture lifestyle has one thing going for it: it provides tomorrow's nostalgia; as soon as things are far enough down memory lane, we invariably start looking at them with enchanted eyes.

The other good thing about nostalgia is that you can recycle the ideas without being accused of petit larceny; people might even admire your interest in things historical. Frederic Goudy once said "The old guys stole all our best ideas" – we could certainly do worse than look to the past for typographic inspiration. After all, most of the typeface styles we now see have been around for a few hundred years, or at least several decades.

Old advertisements are always a source of amusement, and today we have access to digital versions of the typefaces our predecessors used. We can re-create early ads almost faithfully. A note of caution: if you imitate that old look too well, people might not realize that you're actually trying to tell (or sell) them something new.

The fonts used in our nostalgic ad all come from the days of hot metal typesetting, when one typeface would have to serve the printer not only for setting advertisements, but also for things like invitations and stationery. Type was neither cheap nor as easily available as it is today, so a printer's investment had to go a long way.

Berliner Grotesk was designed in Berlin around 1913 as a narrow, fairly light face. What is now the medium weight started out as Block Medium, and was redrawn to match weights and shapes of Berliner Grotesk Light. A bold version is still outstanding.

The Block family is thus related to the Berliners. This relationship is seen not only in the wobbly outlines, but also in some of the idiosyncratic lettershapes.

.Handgloves

BERLINER GROTESK LIGHT

.Handgloves

BERLINER GROTESK MEDIUM

.Handgloves

BLOCK REGULAR

.*Handgloves*

BLOCK ITALIC

.Handgloves

BLOCK CONDENSED

.Handgloves

BLOCK EXTRA CONDENSED

.*Handgloves*

BLOCK EXTRA CONDENSED ITALIC

.**Handgloves**

BLOCK HEAVY

Largest Circulation Anywhere

THE

DAILY INTEREST

Boy Raised by $ea Otters Declared Financial Wizard

NATIONAL EXCLUSIVE

ELVIS SEEN AT BANK

Be ashamed to catch yourself idle. When you have so much to do, be up by the peep of day. Don't let the sun look down and say: "Inglorious here she lays." Handle those tools without mittens; remember, that the cat in gloves catches no mice. It is so true there is much to be done, and perhaps you are weak-handed, but stick to it steadily, and you will see great effects, for constant dropping wears away stones; and by diligence and patience, the mouse ate in two the cable, and little strokes fell great oaks. If you want a faithful servant, and one that you like, serve yourself. Be circumspect and caring, even in the smallest matters, because sometimes a little neglect breeds great mischief: for want of a nail the shoe was lost, for want of a shoe the horse was lost, being soon overtaken and stolen by the enemy, all for want of care of a horse-shoe nail. continued on pg. 12

Aliens Open $1 Million Account in Tucson

Woman Faints While Waiting for Traveler's Checks
"I thought it was my new diet."

Think of saving as well as getting. A person may, if she doesn't know how to save it as she gets it, keep her nose all her life to the grindstone, and die not worth a penny. A fat kitchen does makes a lean will. You may think, perhaps, that a little tea, or a little punch now and then, a diet that's a little more costly, clothes a little finer, and little entertainment now and then, can be no great matter: Many a little makes a mickle; beware of those little expenses – a small leak will sink a great ship, and be reminded again that those who love dainties shall beggars prove, and moreover, fools make feasts, and wise men eat them. Buy what you don't need and before long you will sell your necessities. "At a great penny-worth, pause awhile." Cheapness is apparent only, and not real; the bargain, by straitening you in business,

continued on pg. 12

Every society needs a diversion that doesn't do any physical harm, but keeps those people who prefer to live in fantasy worlds occupied. Certain newspapers cater to this segment of the populace, and the typographic styles reflect their journalistic attitude toward the truth.

How do you design stories about children born with three heads, or families that glow in the dark, or nine-month-old babies who can bench press their moms? Easy: take bold, preferably condensed typefaces, randomly distort the shapes electronically, put outlines around them, mix several together, and insert on the same page.

We haven't quite dared to apply the same techniques in this book. Neither have we exposed our readers to the sort of illustrations these sensationalist newspapers use, although image-manipulation has never been so easy with such realistic results: it's almost too simple to depict a UFO hovering over West Virginia.

Once you start looking for really bold condensed fonts, you realize that among the typefaces in the Adobe type library there aren't that many suited for noisy headlines.

We mentioned the ever-present Futuras, Franklin Gothics, Antique Olives, and Akzidenz Grotesks on page 49, where we also showed Flyer, Block, and Poplar. That is more or less it, except for all the obliques and other variations, and a few others gathered below. Most of these, however, are far too well behaved and good looking to use in a sensationalist way.

. **Handgloves**
AACHEN BOLD

. **Handgloves**
BARMENO EXTRA BOLD

. **Handgloves**
FORMATA BOLD CONDENSED

. **Handgloves**
GOTHIC 13

. **Handgloves**
HELVETICA CONDENSED BLACK

. **Handgloves**
HELVETICA INSERAT

. **Handgloves**
IMPACT

. **Handgloves**
TEMPO HEAVY CONDENSED

If time be of all things the most precious, wasting time must be the greatest prodigality; |

since lost time is never found again, | and what we call time enough always proves little enough. | Let us then be up and doing, and doing to a purpose,

so by diligence we should do more with less perplexity. | Sloth makes all things difficult, but industry all things easy. |

He that riseth late must trot all day and shall scarce overtake the business at night; while laziness travels so slowly

that poverty soon overtakes him. | Sloth, like rust, consumes faster than labor wears, while the used key is always bright. | Do not squander

time, for that's the stuff life is made of; for how much more than is necessary do we spend in sleep, forgetting that there will be sleeping enough in the grave.

So what signifies wishing and hoping for better times? | We may make these times better if we bestir ourselves. | Industry need not wish, and

he that lives upon hope will die fasting. | There are no gains without pains. | He that hath a trade

hath an estate. | Though you have found no treasure, nor has any rich relation left you a legacy, diligence is the mother

of good luck, and all things are given to industry.| Plow deep while sluggards sleep and you will have corn.

Carta

Universal News and Commercial Pi

Letters are things,
not pictures of things.

Eric Gill (1882–1940) was a
sculptor, carver of inscriptional
lettering, wood engraver, book
illustrator, and essayist on
cultural issues. Gill's eccentric
and controversial personal style
continues to be a much talked
about and incongruous element
in his list of considerable accom-
plishments. He designed the
typefaces Gill Sans, Perpetua,
and Joanna.

CHAPTER 6

Types of type

What do we remember about people? Without the aid of sound and scent, we have to rely on the visual data: the color of their eyes and their hair; are they tall or small, slight or heavy; do they wear glasses, have a beard, or crooked teeth?

Many of these features are obscured and thus unavailable for identification purposes when somebody just steps into your path from out of the sun. All you see is an outline, no features. The more clothes this somebody wears, the more the shape is obscured. The worst case is the one we've illustrated here: we asked John, Paul, George, and Rita to wear hats and jackets for these photographs, and consequently had a hard time telling who was who when we looked at the prints.

But then that *was* the point. Typographically speaking, this would be like spelling words in capitals only and then putting a box around each letter. You would have to look at each letter individually to be able to spell the word, and there would be no help from the overall word shapes. Unfortunately, many signs that we are supposed to be able to read in passing are designed this way. But words are like faces: the more features we can see, the easier it is to tell who is who.

While we have made things difficult by only using capitals and putting those into a box, we at least used a typeface that is easy to read; the letterforms are distinct enough to tell them apart, while not so individual that it's hard to read complete words.

When we read longer text, we don't look at individual characters; we recognize whole word shapes and see what we expect to see. That's why we don't often spot typing errors. But when we are looking for something new or unknown, like the name of a place or a person, we need to look at each letter carefully. This is particularly true for checking names or numbers in telephone books or other directories. The typefaces designed for these purposes (shown on page 37) give prominence to individual characters. For text fonts, the art is creating clear, distinguishable letterforms that harmonize well in words and sentences.

The big test words in boxes are set in Myriad; below are alternative sans serif capitals.

JOHN **PAUL**

GEORGE **RITA**

GEORGE
ITC Avant Garde Gothic Demi

GEORGE
Gill Sans Bold

GEORGE
DIN Mittelschrift

GEORGE
Futura Heavy

GEORGE
Akzidenz Grotesk Medium

GEORGE
Helvetica Bold

Since it's polite to take off one's hat when meeting someone, we now have a chance to get a better look at our four well-mannered friends: still no faces, but different hairstyles give us better clues to their identities.

Setting the names in capitals and lower case gives each of the words a definite outline. If you look at them again, you could probably tell them apart just by the shape of the box, at least that is what your subconscious will do: if it sees a similar shape, it will automatically give you the name associated with it.

The outline of a word is determined by which letters jut up from the main body and which hang down. They are called ascenders and descenders, respectively.

Research has shown that our eyes scan the top of the letters' x-heights during the normal reading process, so that is where the primary identification of each letter takes place. The brain assembles the information and compares it with the shape of the word's outline. If we had to consciously look at individual letters all the time, we would read as slowly as children who have not learned to assume a word's meaning from such minimal information.

While ascenders and descenders are vital for easy reading, they have to blend in so they don't attract attention to themselves. Typefaces with exaggerated details may look very attractive word by word, but are their own worst enemies when it comes to unimpeded reading. In typography, everything is connected to everything else; individual elements are noticeable only at the expense of the whole.

The test words on the left are set in capital and lowercase Myriad. Below are ascenders and descenders, as performed by four other typefaces.

George & Paul
Antique Olive (hardly any ascenders or descenders)

George & Paul
ITC Garamond Book (not very explicit)

George & Paul
Stempel Garamond (average)

George & Paul
Weiss Italic (pretty obvious ascenders)

The moment of truth, in life as in typography: no more hiding behind hats or coming in from the light. Now we can look at features – eyes, lips, hair – as well as man-made additions like beards, glasses, and haircuts. And our friends have expressions on their faces, although they were all told to look normal.

Obviously that meant something different to each of them, as it does when typefaces are described as normal, useful, or sturdy, let alone beautiful, delicate, or handsome.

Most graphic designers and typographers agree that only a handful of typefaces is needed for their daily work; fortunately (at least for the manufacturers and type designers), they could never agree on the same dozen or so typefaces. We need thousands. Then each of us can pick our favorites. Just like shoes: one doesn't need more than half a dozen pairs, but another person will make a different selection, and so on. For individual expression, as well as maximum legibility, we need to pull out all the stops.

Picking the right font for a particular message can be fun, but also extremely difficult. What do you want to express besides the bare facts? How much do you want to interpret, add your own comment, decorate, illustrate? Even if you choose what might be called a "neutral" typeface, you've made a choice that tells people the message is neutral.

When you design the visual appearance of a message, you are adding some interpretation to it. John, Paul, George, and Rita would doubtless have a lively discussion about the typefaces chosen to represent their names and thus, them.

The choices were governed not so much by trying to get across their personalities, as by the actual letters appearing in their names. Choosing a typeface to set a word in is part of manipulating the meaning of that word.

John

Gill Sans Bold

Paul

Tekton Bold

George

Concorde Nova Medium

Rita

ITC Benguiat Gothic Bold

It is one thing to pick typefaces to represent individual people, and quite another to express similarities as well as differences within the same family. We know that sisters and brothers don't always get along with each other. However, it is easy to tell when people belong to the same family; some take after the father, some after the mother, and some have a combination of both parents' features.

Type also comes in families. While some of the weights might be used more extensively than others (you wouldn't set a whole book in semibold type), there is no paternal or maternal dominance within typographic families. Each member does his or her work regardless of sex, age, or status. In some respects, the world of type is an ideal one.

The Trapp family demonstrated old-fashioned family values: live together, sing together.

Traditionally, typefaces used for setting books had no bold weights, let alone extrabold or condensed versions, or even real display weights. Those more eye-catching additions came about at the beginning of the nineteenth century, when the Industrial Revolution created the need to advertise goods.

Properly applied, however, a complete family gives you enough scope to solve all typographic tasks in the setting of text. Nowadays, semibold or bold weights are part of even the most traditional families.

If you find that incestuous typography won't solve your communication problem, you can go outside and bring in some fresh blood from other families. These days, this is quite permissible – more about that on page 101.

The Adobe Garamond family was designed in 1989 by Robert Slimbach. Without its small capitals, and bold and italic children, and its titling cousin, this typographic family wouldn't be large enough to form a choir.

.Handgloves
ADOBE GARAMOND REGULAR

.*Handgloves*
ADOBE GARAMOND ITALIC

.Handgloves
ADOBE GARAMOND SEMIBOLD

.*Handgloves*
ADOBE GARAMOND SEMI. ITAL.

.**Handgloves**
ADOBE GARAMOND BOLD

.***Handgloves***
ADOBE GARAMOND BOLD ITALIC

.HANDGLOVES
ADOBE GARAMOND TITLING

.HANDGLOVES
ADOBE GARAMOND EXPERT

.**HANDGLOVES**
ADOBE GARAMOND EXP. SEMI.

Can you tell the difference between a National steel guitar, a square-neck Hawaiian, a Fender Telecaster, a Dreadnought, or an acoustic twelve-string? Look to your left. Some of those guitars are there, lined up in the livingroom of the musician who let us take this photograph. To play a wide variety of music, all of these guitars are needed.

Even though only serious musicians could detect the difference between instruments on a recording, the guitarist still has to decide which one will make the particular piece sound perfect, just as a chef will use spices you've never heard of to make your supper taste wonderful. It's the adaptation of one basic, popular tool to serve many different purposes, and the professional needs all the choices available.

Type is no exception when it comes to refinement. Not surprisingly, the fonts providing that extra something are called "expert sets." Some of them do indeed require an expert to find all the right characters and put them in the proper place, but if you have a complex problem to solve, you cannot expect simple solutions.

Remember the typewriter? It has fewer keys than a computer keyboard, and the most you could get on your golfball or daisywheel were 96 characters. Considering that the alphabet only has 26 letters, that isn't bad, but compare it to the full character set of around 220 characters in a typical digital font.

There are languages other than English, measurements other than inches, feet, and yards. Specialized professions and sciences require their own ways of encoding and decoding messages and expert sets make this a little easier. Two types of characters that used to be part of standard typeface families are now found in expert sets: old style figures and ligatures.

Numbers can be an eyesore when they are set in the middle of regular text. Old style figures, sometimes called lowercase figures, are endowed with features like ascenders and descenders, which allow them to blend right in with the other words on a page. Sometimes, a letter collides with a part of a neighboring one. The most obvious example is the overhang on the *f* and the dot on the *i*. Combination characters, called ligatures, prevent that unhappy collision.

fi fl ff ffi ffl

fi fl ff ffi ffl

Left: Before and after ligatures.

Right: Expert fonts are available for many popular and practical typefaces; this increases their usefulness beyond everyday jobs. Adobe Expert sets include small capitals, fractions, ligatures, special characters, and old style figures.

ABCDEFGHIJKLMN
OPQRSTUVWXY&Z
¼ ½ ⅛ ⅜ ⅝ ⅔
ff fi ffi ffl fl
Å Ž Ý Rp ¢ $ ^ .. Ý
1234567890

What if some members of your family can't sing? What if you need two sopranos, but only have one sister? Maybe you have three sisters and two brothers who can't sing or play an instrument. Okay, then find yourself some outsiders, put them in the same sort of outfits, call them a "family" and everybody will believe you've been together all your lives. This is what Lawrence Welk did.

The typographic equivalent does not appear quite so harmonious. In fact, the idea is to bring in outside fonts which do things your basic family can't. Usually this means a few more heavy weights if you're setting text in a classic book typeface that hasn't got a bold, let alone an extrabold weight. Or you might need more contrast – magazine pages all set in one kind of type tend to look very gray. And then, some fonts look better in certain sizes, so this too has to be considered if you have text that has to be set much smaller or larger.

High fashion designers call these things *accessoires*, and typographic equivalents have to be chosen the same way: they have to fulfill a particular function while achieving an aesthetic balance with the main dress.

The best way to add typographic impact is to use extended typeface families such as Lucida, which include a sans serif and a serif; or a family such as ITC Stone, which has a sans serif, a serif, and an informal version.

The latest and most ambitious addition to the these universal families is Agfa Rotis, designed in 1989 by Otl Aicher, one of Germany's best-known designers. Rotis is the name of a small village in the Alps; the typeface exists in four versions: Sans, Semisans, Semiserif, and Serif.

A more daring way to add contrast and adventure to a typographic page is to invite members from other typeface families. It is generally all right to mix different types from the same designer (Eric Gill's Joanna and Gill Sans work well together, as do most of Adrian Frutiger's types), or from the same period, or even very different periods. There are almost as many recipes as there are fonts. The pages in this book are themselves examples of mixing different typefaces: Minion multiple master for text; and Myriad multiple master, a sans serif in a bold weight at a smaller size (and in a second color) for sidebars, and another weight for captions.

.Handgloves

AGFA ROTIS SANS SERIF

.Handgloves

AGFA ROTIS SEMISANS

.Handgloves

AGFA ROTIS SERIF

.Handgloves

JOANNA REGULAR

.Handgloves

JOANNA SEMIBOLD

.Handgloves

JOANNA BOLD

.**Handgloves**

JOANNA EXTRA BOLD

.Handgloves

GILL SANS REGULAR

.*Handgloves*

GILL SANS REGULAR ITALIC

.**Handgloves**

GILL SANS BOLD

.*Handgloves*

GILL SANS BOLD ITALIC

Now that we've started the music/type comparison, let's use one more example from that world to illustrate another typographic feature.

There is loud music and quiet music, dulcet tones and heavy ones, and there is – did you ever doubt it? – a typographic parallel. Some typefaces are loud by design, some are rather fine and sweet. A good family of fonts will cater to all these moods.

To illustrate the widest possible range within one family, we've chosen the typeface of many weights and versions, Helvetica, beginning with the lightest weights to suggest the tones of a flute. Very light typefaces are for those messages we want to look delicate and elegant.

Helvetica is not the most elegant type design of all time, but it is practical and objective, and it is seen everywhere. Designed by Max Miedinger in 1957, the family grew in leaps and bounds with different typefoundries (Haas in Switzerland, Stempel and Linotype in Germany) adding weights as their customers created the demand for them. The result was a large family that didn't look very related.

When digital type became the production standard, Linotype decided to reissue the entire Helvetica family, this time coordinating all the versions to cover as many weights and widths as possible. To help distinguish among the fifty of them, they were given the same numbering system as the one devised by Adrian Frutiger for Univers (see page 79); the lightest weight is designated by a "2" in its name. The typeface has been renamed Neue (German for "new") Helvetica.

HHHHHHHH

25   26   35   36   45   46   55   56

The flute makes light, delicate sounds; on the other end of the musical spectrum with its undeniably substantial sound is the tuba. As every music lover knows, a big instrument doesn't always need to be played at full volume, and a tuba will never work in the confines of a string quartet.

There are also limits to the use of very bold typefaces. At small sizes the spaces inside bold letters start filling in, making most words illegible. So, like writing music for the tuba, the best thing for bold faces is to use them where you need to accentuate rhythm and lend emphasis to the other instruments and voices.

As letters get bolder, the white space inside them decreases, making them appear smaller than lighter counterparts. The type designer has to allow for this effect by slightly increasing the height of bolder letters. A similar thing occurs with the width of the letter – as the thickness of the stems increases, weight has to be added to the outsides of the letters, making the bolder weights wider than their lighter cousins.

By the time letters are very bold, they're usually called black or heavy, or even extra black or ultra black. There is no system for naming weights in a family, so for clear communication it is safer to use the number designations when talking about a large family like Neue Helvetica.

Once the weight of a letter has reached a certain critical mass and width, it begins to look extended, as well as extra bold. Extending a design adds white space to the counters (the space inside letters), so some extended black versions may appear lighter than their narrower black counterparts.

In the case of Neue Helvetica, there is one more weight beyond the 95 (black) version: 107, extra black condensed. If you look very closely you will notice, however, that the width of the stems is no wider than that of the black weight. Condensing letter shapes makes the internal spaces smaller and the type much darker.

.**Handgloves**

65 NEUE HELVETICA MEDIUM

.**Handgloves**

75 NEUE HELVETICA BOLD

.**Handgloves**

85 NEUE HELVETICA HEAVY

.**Handgloves**

95 NEUE HELVETICA BLACK

.**Handgloves**

107 NEUE HELVETICA
EXTRA BLACK CONDENSED

HᴴHᴴHᴴHᴴH

65   66   75   76   85   86   95   96

23   24   33   34   43   44   53   54   63   64   83   84

Rhythm and contrast keep coming up when discussing good music and good typographic design. They are concepts that also apply to spoken language, as anyone who has had to sit through a monotonous lecture will attest; the same tone, volume, and speed of speech will put even the most interested listener into dreamland. Every now and again the audience needs to be shaken, either by a change in voice or pitch, by a question being posed, or by the speaker talking very quietly and then suddenly shouting. An occasional joke also works, just as the use of a funny typeface can liven up a page.

There's only one thing worse than a badly told joke, and that is a joke told twice. Whatever typographic device you come up with, don't let it turn into a gimmick. A well-coordinated range of fonts will give you the scope for contrast as well as rhythm, and will keep you secure in the bosom of a well-behaved family.

Unlike Univers, Neue Helvetica does not have extremely condensed weights, but within the traditional family of Helveticas there are dozens of other versions, from Helvetica Inserat to compressed or even extra and ultra compressed weights.

Changing the typographic rhythm by the occasional use of a condensed or, indeed, extended typeface can work wonders. Remember, however, that space problems should never be solved by setting long copy in a very condensed face.

Although large families such as Helvetica can make your typographic life easy, it won't be long before they become predictable; the proverb "Jack of all trades, master of none" comes to mind. One would be foolish to ignore the special fonts that have been developed to solve particular problems.

If you want ultimate variety within one formal framework, turn to the next page.

. Handgloves

HELVETICA INSERAT

. Handgloves

HELVETICA COMPRESSED

. Handgloves

HELVETICA EXTRA COMPRESSED

. Handgloves

HELVETICA ULTRA COMPRESSED

/H H H H H H H H H H H H H H H H

| 37 | 38 | 47 | 48 | 57 | 58 | 67 | 68 | 77 | 78 | 87 | 88 | 97 | 98 | 107 | 108 |

You can have as many bands, groups, combos, quartets, and quintets as you like, but nothing surpasses a full orchestra when it comes to producing all the sounds a composer can dream up. Generally, orchestra musicians use instruments that have remained largely unchanged for several hundred years; however, nowadays the odd modern instrument might be included.

Again, all a little like typography. The instruments (our letters) have been around in very much the same shape for several hundred years, and the tunes (our language) haven't changed beyond recognition either. For classical page designs, we have traditional typefaces and our tried and true ways of arranging them on the page. Even new, experimental layouts work well with those fonts, just as modern composers can realize most of their works with a classical orchestra.

Multiple master typefaces, however, take this comparison one large step further and essentially redefine the way we use typefaces. No more static, prescribed weights and versions, but a nearly unlimited choice of typographic expression within the same framework.

These typefaces are called multiple masters because two or more sets of master designs are integrated into each typeface. These master designs determine what is known as the dynamic range of each design axis. The intermediate font variations are generated by on-demand interpolation between the master designs. For example, a light and a black master design delineate the range of possible weight variations along the weight axis; you can select a font weight anywhere within this range and then "create" the font variation you choose.

A multiple master typeface can have several design axes, including weight, width, style, and optical size (see the next page). Besides a weight axis, Myriad, the first multiple master typeface, also has a width axis, so it can be interpolated between condensed and extended, as well as between light and black. The dynamic range, therefore, extends (no pun intended) from Light Condensed to Black Semi-extended.

We created thirteen fonts of Myriad multiple master for the inside of this book; there are two more on the cover.

Light Condensed   Light Semi-Extended

A simple multiple master design matrix. The four corners represent the master designs.

Black Condensed   Black Semi-Extended

Ergonomics can be defined as the examination of difficulties people have adjusting to their environment, or as the science that seeks to adapt working conditions to better suit the worker. People suffer if chairs are too low, tables too high, lights too dim, or if computer screens have too little contrast or emit too much radiation.

Children could tell stories about having to sit at adult tables, clutching forks that are far too big for them and having to drink from glasses they cannot get their little hands around.

This is what was done to many typefaces since the introduction of the pantograph in the late 1800s; the practice became even more prevalent with the advent of phototypesetting in the mid-1960s. One size had to fit all. One drawing was used to reproduce everything, from very small type to headline-size type and beyond. The multiple master optical size axis makes it possible to bring out the variations in design details that allow a typeface to be readable at different sizes.

Typographic ergonomics at last.

Hmfg
6-point

Hmfg
72-point

Compare the differences between the letter shapes and overall weight of the above letters. The 6-point design has heavier stems and serifs, wider characters, and a larger x-height.

When type was made out of metal (see page 53), each size had to be designed differently and cut separately. The engraver knew from experience what had to be done to make each size highly readable. On very small type, hairlines were a little heavier so they would not only be easier to read, but also not break under pressure from the printing press.

When one master design is used to fit all sizes, as in phototypesetting and digital systems, these subtleties are lost, resulting in compromises that very often gave type designs a bad name. This is especially true in the re-creations of classic faces: when originally designed, there was a limited range of sizes acceptable from both readability and aesthetic standpoints.

Minion multiple master has an optical size axis which makes it possible to generate fonts that are optically adjusted for use at specific point sizes: the text sizes are clear and easy to read, and display sizes are refined and elegant.

Minion multiple master was designed in 1991 by Robert Slimbach, who was inspired by old style typefaces of the late Renaissance. You can form your own opinion of this type and its italic companion, as well as its expert set, by looking at the main text in this book. We created thirteen fonts of Minion for the inside, and fourteen for the cover.

Anyone who would letterspace
lower case would steal sheep.

Frederic Goudy (1894–1945),
American typographer and type
designer, did not design his first
typeface until he was forty-five.
He is noted for his profusion of
innovative and eclectic type
designs and his forthright
declarations on typographic
issues.

CHAPTER 7

How it works

Letters were originally invented to help communicate not high culture, but mundane things like the amount of goods delivered or their value in barter or currency. What began as individual signs representing real items developed into letters and alphabets.

Different cultures added to the typographic variety. For instance, the most common vowel sound in ancient languages was also the the first letter of the alphabet. The Phoenicians (ca. 1000 BC) called it aleph, the Greeks (ca. 500 BC), alpha, the Romans (ca. 50 BC) ah. The Phoenicians had twenty-two letters in their alphabet; the Greeks added vowels, and the Romans developed the letters we still use today. All this time, people wrote either from right to left, or left to right, or top to bottom.

With such a mixed history, no wonder our alphabet looks so unbalanced. Anyone inventing a new alphabet today would doubtless be more practical and make letters more regular. There would be more obvious differences between some shapes, and no narrow letters such as *l* in the same alphabet with wide ones such as *m*.

One consequence of our letters having such complex yet delicate shapes is that we have to respect their space. Every one of them needs enough room on both sides to avoid clashes with its neighbors. The smaller the type, the more space that's needed on the sides. Only big, robust headlines can have the occasional letter very close to the next one.

Tree farms are to forests what monospaced fonts are to real type.

The history of type is also a history of technical constraints. Mechanical typewriters gave us monospaced fonts. Each letter had the same amount of lateral space, regardless of its shape. Later developments led to fonts with more regular letter shapes; this did not necessarily improve legibility, but these alphabets no longer had any gaps between characters. They also appear extremely readable to computers, who don't care that much about tradition.

As soon as typewriters got little computers inside them, they were able to set justified text (lines of the same length), a style which was, and is, totally unnecessary in office communication. But people had learned from reading newspapers, magazines, and books that this was how type should be set.

Now technology allows us to typeset most of the alphabets ever created and actually improve on their appearance, definition, and arrangement. Proportionately spaced fonts are easier to read, occupy less space, allow for more expression, and are nicer to look at. The only reason to still use monospaced fonts is to imitate the time-honored and personal look of typewriters.

In monospaced typewriter typefaces, every letter occupies the same lateral space: the *i* is stretched on the rack, while the *m* suffers claustrophobia. The most common measurements are 12 characters to the inch (12-pitch) or 10 to the inch (10-pitch).

115

Looking at nature, we imagine that God could have designed more practical forests than the ones we know: they are difficult to get around in, full of different kinds of trees in various stages of growth, and there's not enough light. Luckily, we humans are also part of this wonderful, if not entirely perfect system called nature; we like things that look "human" (less than perfect), but we also like that things conform to a master plan, even if it is indecipherable. We know when something looks "right" without ever having to measure it.

Unfortunately, people have long since begun improving on creation. We won't go into a discussion of inventions like nuclear power or low-fat dog food, but certainly tree farms are a good example of what some people think nature should look like. If we applied the same logic to type, we wouldn't have any unusual or eccentric designs, where every letter has a different shape and its own individual space. Instead there would only be regularized fonts with nice geometrically defined shapes. How mundane our typographic lives would be.

Unsightly character combinations are remedied with kerning.

There are sometimes unsightly gaps that occur between and around particular combinations of letters. Obvious problem letters are V, W, and Y in both capitals and lower case. Other bad gaps appear between numbers and periods or commas, particularly after a 7. (Just like this.)

Once you look into the relationship of two or more characters in a word, you realize what a mess it can be – not unlike other relationships. One of the most often-spoken words in desktop typography makes its appearance at this point: *kerning*. To get rid of these gaps, one simply removes the space (or maybe adds it) between the offending pair of letters. A certain number of these problem combinations are adjusted by the type designer; they are known as "kerning pairs" and are included in font programs.

Tracking controls the space between letters globally; this means that equal amounts of space can be added between every letter in your text. It is here that Mr. Goudy's dictum reminds us of the impending danger: as the space between letters increases, so does the difficulty comprehending single words, and thus the thoughts conveyed in our text.

To Tr Ve Wo

To Tr Ve Wo

r. y, 7. w -

r. y, 7. w-

Letters, like trees, hardly ever appear by themselves. As soon as there are a bunch of letters gathered together, they fight for space, for the right to be recognized, to be read. If you plant trees too close together, they'll struggle to get light and for space for their roots to expand; the weaker ones will stop growing and eventually die.

Before this turns into a tale of typographic Darwinism, let's look at the practical consequences as far as this book and its typographic subject is concerned. If you know your text is going to be fairly long and that it will require some time to read, you should adjust the layout accordingly. The lines should be long enough to get complete thoughts into them and there ought to be enough space between them to be able to finish reading one line before your eye gets distracted by the next.

Marathon runners know they have twenty-six miles ahead of them, so it would be foolish to start off like crazy. There is also no need to run in narrow tracks, since by the time everybody gets settled into the race there will be plenty of room, with the first runners miles away from the last ones. With thousands of people in the race, individuals will blend into the crowd, but they still have to give their best.

Long texts require a setting not unlike the way a marathon is run. Everything has to be comfortable – once you've found your rhythm, nothing must disturb it again. If you have text that is going to require long-distance reading, design it so the reader has a chance to settle in. The rhythm depends on the spacing contingencies below.

Letters need to be far enough apart to be distinguished from one another, but not so far that they separate into individual, unrelated signs. Mr. Goudy knew what he was talking about.

Word spaces have to be gauged so the reader is able to see individual words, but also to group them together for quick comprehension.

The space between lines of type has to be generous enough to prevent the eye from slipping to the next line before it is finished gathering information in the current one.

The text below has been set for comfortable long-distance reading.

If time be of all things the most precious, wasting time must be the greatest prodigality; since lost time is never found again, and what we call time enough always proves little enough. Let us then be up and doing, and doing to a purpose, so by diligence we should do more with less perplexity. Sloth makes all things difficult, but industry all things easy. He that riseth late must trot all day and shall scarce overtake the business at night; while laziness travels so slowly that poverty soon overtakes him. Sloth, like rust, consumes faster than labor wears, while the used key is always bright. Do not squander time, for that's the stuff

What did people do before there was the instant replay? The 100-yard dash is over in less than ten seconds these days, and we can't possibly look at each of the six or more contestants by the time they're across the line.

Does that sound like thumbing through a magazine, with all those ads flashing by your eyes in split seconds? That's typography at its most intense. If you want to make an impression in an ad, you can't wait for the readers to get settled in, and there is no space to spread your message out in front of their eyes. The sprinter has to hurl forward, and stay in a narrow lane. In short-distance text, lines have to be short and compact or the reader's eye will be drawn to the next line before reaching the end of the previous one.

Setting text in short lines for quick scanning requires rearrangement of all the other parameters, too. Tracking can be tighter, and word spaces and line spaces smaller.

The choice of typefaces is, of course, another consideration. A type that invites you to read long copy has to be inconspicuous and self-effacing, confirming our acquired prejudice about what is readable. A quick look at a short piece of writing could be assisted by a typeface that has a little verve. It shouldn't be as elaborate as a display font used on a label or a poster, but it also doesn't need to be too modest.

If time be of all things the most precious, wasting time must be the greatest prodigality; since lost time is never found again, and what we call time enough always proves little enough. Let us then be up and doing, and doing to a purpose, so by diligence we should do more with less perplexity. Sloth makes all things difficult, but industry all things easy. He that riseth late must trot all day and shall scarce overtake the business at night; while laziness travels so slowly that poverty soon overtakes him. Sloth, like rust, consumes faster than labor wears, while the used key is always bright. Do not squander time, for that's the stuff life is made of; how much more than is necessary do we spend in sleep,

The above text has been tuned for sprint reading. Compare the long-distance text from the previous page.

While driving on freeways isn't quite as exhausting as running a marathon (mainly because you get to sit down in your car), it requires a similar mind-set. The longer the journey, the more relaxed your driving style should be. You know you're going to be on the road for a while, and it's best not to get too nervous, but sit back, keep a safe distance from the car in front of you, and cruise.

Long-distance reading needs a relaxed attitude, too. There is nothing worse than having to get used to a different set of parameters every other line: compare it to the jarring effect of a fellow motorist who suddenly appears in front of you, having jumped a lane just to gain twenty yards. Words should also keep a safe, regular distance from each other, so that you can rely on the next one to appear when you're ready for it.

The tricky thing about space is that it is generally invisible and therefore easy to ignore. At night you can see only as far as the headlights of your car can shine. You determine your speed by the size of the visible space in front of you.

It used to be a rule of thumb for headline settings to leave a space between words that is just wide enough to fit in a lowercase *i*. For comfortable reading of long lines, the space between words should be much wider. The default settings in most software vary these values, but the normal 100 percent word space seems just fine for lines of at least ten words (or just over fifty characters). Shorter lines always require tighter word space (more about that on the following page).

The iway ito iwealth

If time be of all things the most precious, wasting time must be the greatest prodigality; since lost time is never found again, and what we call time enough always proves little enough. Let us then be up and doing, and doing to a purpose, so by diligence we should do more

If time be of all things the most precious, wasting time must be the greatest prodigality; since lost time is never found again, and what we call time enough always proves little enough. Let us then be up and doing, and doing to a purpose, so by diligence we should do more

A lowercase *i* makes a nice word space for headlines. Short lines should have modest space between the words.

You must have noticed that the lanes on the freeway are wider than those on city streets, even though cars are the same size on both types of roads. But when traveling at high speeds, every movement of the steering wheel can cause a major deviation from the straight lane you're supposed to be driving in, posing a threat to other drivers.

This is, in typographic words, not the space between words, but that between lines – the lanes that words drive in. Typographic details and refinement relate to everything else; if you increase your word space, you have to have more space between the lines as well.

One rule to remember about line space is that it needs to be larger than the space between words, otherwise your eye would be inclined to travel from the word on the first line directly to the word on the line below. When line space is correct your eye will first make the journey along one line before it continues on to the next.

The rest is very simple: the more words per line, the more space needed between the lines. You can then increase the space *ever so slightly* between the letters (that is, track them) as the lines get longer.

If time be of all things the most precious, wasting time must be the greatest prodigality; since lost time is never found again, and what we call time enough always proves little enough. Let us then be up and doing, and doing to a purpose, so by diligence we should do more with less perplexity. Sloth makes all things difficult, but industry all things easy. He that riseth late must trot all day and shall scarce overtake the business at night; while laziness travels so slowly that poverty soon overtakes him. Sloth, like rust, consumes faster than labor wears, while the used key is always bright. Do not squander time, for that's the stuff life is made of; how much more than is necessary do we spend in sleep, forgetting that the sleeping fox catches no poultry, and that there will be sleeping enough in the grave. So what signifies wishing and hoping for better times? We may make these times better if we bestir ourselves. Industry need not wish, and he that lives upon hope will die fasting. There are no gains without pains. He that has a trade has an estate, and he that has a calling has an office of profit and honor. But then the trade must be worked at and the calling honored. But then the trade

The miracle of computers has enabled line spaces to be adjusted in very small increments. In this example, none

of the other parameters has changed – tracking and word space remain the same but the line space increases.

Notice how the more widely spaced lines cry out for looser tracking and wider word spaces.

In both life and typography, the object is to get safely and quickly from A to B. What is safe at sixty miles an hour on a straight freeway with four lanes in good daylight would be suicide in city traffic. You have to adjust your driving to the road conditions, and you have to adjust typographic parameters to the conditions of the page and the purpose of the message.

Whether you're driving along looking at the scenery, or stuck in a traffic jam, or slowly moving from one set of lights to the next, you have to be conscious of the drivers around you. If they change their behavior, you have to react. When you learn the rules and have had a little practice, nothing will upset you, not in traffic and not in typography.

One of the best ways to keep the reader's attention on the content of your message is to keep the color of the printed text consistent. Newspapers do a very bad job of it. They agree that type, even in narrow columns, has to be justified. The result is words and lines that are erratically letter-spaced. Readers have become used to that style (or rather, lack of it); loose and tight lines of type, one after another, don't seem to upset anyone.

In other surroundings, however, lines that look a little lighter and then a little darker because no one has adjusted the spacing might make the reader think there is some purpose behind this arrangement: are the loose lines more important than the tight ones?

Again, and there is no guarantee this is the last time: every time you change one spacing parameter, you have to look closely at all the others and adjust them accordingly.

Longer lines need wider spaces: in these examples, line space, tracking, and word spaces have all been increased as the lines got wider.

If time be of all things the most precious, wasting time must be the greatest prodigality; since lost time is never found again, and what we call time enough always proves little enough. Let us then be up and doing, and doing to a purpose, so by diligence we

If time be of all things the most precious, wasting time must be the greatest prodigality; since lost time is never found again, and what we call time enough always proves little enough. Let us then be up and doing, and doing to a purpose, so by diligence we should do more with less perplexity.

If time be of all things the most precious, wasting time must be the greatest prodigality; since lost time is never found again, and what we call time enough always proves little enough. Let us then be up and doing, and doing to a purpose, so by diligence we should do more with less perplexity. Sloth makes all

There are situations, and this really is the final car picture, in which normal rules don't apply. Space becomes a rare commodity indeed when thousands of people are trying to get to the same place at the same time. Some pages are just like a downtown traffic jam: too many messages, too many directions, and too much noise.

One thing typography can do, however, that city planning cannot: we can make all of our vehicles different sizes, move them up and down, overlap them, put them into the background, or turn them sideways. A page like this looks better than your typical downtown gridlock.

If time be of all things the most precious, wasting time must be the greatest prodigality; since lost time is never found again, and what we call time enough always proves little enough. Let us then be up and doing, and doing to a purpose, so by diligence we should do more with less perplexity. Sloth makes all things difficult, but industry all things easy. He that riseth late must trot all day and shall scarce overtake the business at night; while laziness travels so slowly that poverty soon overtakes him. Sloth, like rust, consumes faster than labor wears, while the used key is always bright.

This copy is set to the same specifications as the second example on page 131, but reversed out.

If time be of all things the most precious, wasting time must be the greatest prodigality; since lost time is never found again, and what we call time enough always proves little enough. Let us then be up and doing, and doing to a purpose, so by diligence we should do more with less perplexity. Sloth makes all things difficult, but industry all things easy. He that riseth late must trot all day and shall scarce overtake the business at night; while laziness travels so slowly that poverty soon overtakes him. Sloth, like rust, consumes faster than labor wears, while the used key is always bright.

In reversed-out settings, the spaces between letters look smaller, because they are dark. This text is set with the letterspacing (tracking) more open than the example above.

If time be of all things the most precious, wasting time must be the greatest prodigality; since lost time is never found again, and what we call time enough always proves little enough. Let us then be up and doing, and doing to a purpose, so by diligence we should do more with less perplexity. Sloth makes all things difficult, but industry all things easy. He that riseth late must trot all day and shall scarce overtake the business at night; while laziness travels so slowly that poverty soon overtakes him. Sloth, like rust, consumes faster than labor wears, while the used key is always bright.

White type looks heavier than black type (dark color recedes, bright colors come forward), so we created an instance of Minion multiple master that was lighter in weight.

If time be of all things the most precious, wasting time must be the greatest prodigality; since lost time is never found again, and what we call time enough always proves little enough. Let us then be up and doing, and doing to a purpose, so by diligence we should do more with less perplexity. Sloth makes all things difficult, but industry all things easy. He that riseth late must trot all day and shall scarce overtake the business at night; while laziness travels so slowly that poverty soon overtakes him. Sloth, like rust, consumes faster than labor wears, while the used key is always bright.

Often the problem is not that white type looks too heavy, but that the ink-spread from the printing process fills in the open spaces in and around letters. We have chosen a smaller optical size of Minion multiple master to make it a little sturdier.

1

If time be of all things the most precious, wasting time must be the greatest prodigality; since lost time is never found again, and what we call time enough always proves little enough. Let us then be up and doing, and doing to a purpose, so by diligence we should do more with less perplexity. Sloth makes all things difficult, but industry all things easy. He that riseth late must trot all day and shall scarce overtake the business at night; while laziness travels so slowly that poverty soon overtakes him. Sloth, like rust, consumes faster than labor wears, while the used key is always bright.

Remember: the more letters contained in a line, the more space that's needed between words and lines.

2

If time be of all things the most precious, wasting time must be the greatest prodigality; since lost time is never found again, and what we call time enough always proves little enough. Let us then be up and doing, and doing to a purpose, so by diligence we should do more with less perplexity. Sloth makes all things difficult, but industry all things easy. He that riseth late must trot all day and shall scarce overtake the business at night; while laziness travels so slowly that poverty soon overtakes him. Sloth, like rust, consumes faster than labor wears, while the used key is always bright.

For comparison among the various settings, the horizontal and vertical scales are broken down into millimeter units.

3

If time be of all things the most precious, wasting time must be the greatest prodigality; since lost time is never found again, and what we call time enough always proves little enough. Let us then be up and doing, and doing to a purpose, so by diligence we should do more with less perplexity. Sloth makes all things difficult, but industry all things easy. He that riseth late must trot all day and shall scarce overtake the business at night; while laziness travels so slowly that poverty soon overtakes him. Sloth, like rust, consumes faster than labor wears, while the used key is always bright.

4

If time be of all things the most precious, wasting time must be the greatest prodigality; since lost time is never found again, and what we call time enough always proves little enough. Let us then be up and doing, and doing to a purpose, so by diligence we should do more with less perplexity. Sloth makes all things difficult, but industry all things easy. He that riseth late must trot all day and shall scarce overtake the business at night; while laziness travels so slowly that poverty soon overtakes him. Sloth, like rust, consumes faster than labor wears, while the used key is always bright.

The first example has approximately 4 words (25 characters) per line and is set in 8-point type with 9-point line space (set 8 on 9); word spaces are very small and tracking is very loose. The second example accommodates 8 words (45 characters), is set 8 on 8; word spaces are 10 percent wider and tracking is loose. The third block of text is set 8 on 11, with about 10 words (58 characters) to a line; the word space is opened another 10 percent, and the tracking is a little tighter. The fourth text block is set 8 on 12, and with 15 words (90 characters), which is almost too wide. The word spaces are now at the default value, with a little tracking.

Symmetry is static – that is to say quiet; that is to say, inconspicuous.

William Addison Dwiggins (1880–1956) was a typographer, type designer, puppeteer, and author. The American book trade owes a debt to Dwiggins for bringing style and good design sense into mainstream publishing, most notably with the work he did on Borzoi books. He is responsible for reintroducing colophon pages, which give details about a book's typography and fascinating facts about the typefaces used. Caledonia, Metro, and Elektra are Dwiggins typeface designs.

CHAPTER 8

Putting it to work

The bed is one piece of furniture that has escaped most design trends. Mattresses have changed and so has the technology of making bed frames, but the way we sleep is still the same and the basic bedroom looks the same as it has for centuries.

Bedrooms and books have one thing in common: an essentially single purpose. Reading, like sleeping, hasn't changed much in several hundred years, although we now have reading glasses, electrically operated headrests, and little lamps that clip right onto our books.

It can be said that the forerunner of what we consider coffee table books existed in the early days of printing, showing small illustrations positioned in a narrow marginal column next to the main body of text. Paperbacks crammed full of poorly spaced type with narrow page margins are an unfortunate and fairly recent innovation. But the intimate process of reading a book remains largely unchanged, and so does the look of our books.

Common to every book design is the underlying grid that divides the page into areas that serve different purposes – columns of text, marginal comments, headlines, footnotes, captions, illustrations. The more complex the structure of the text, the more possibilities for the arrangement of elements supported by this grid. Linear reading (as in a novel) usually just needs a straightforward, single-column layout, for which there are plenty of successful historical precedents.

The size of a book is crucial, but is often determined by technical or marketing constraints. Books for serious reading should fit in our hands; it is preferable then to have a narrow format with wide margins that allow room for fingers to hold the book.

The column width (i.e., the length of a line of type) is governed by the width of the page, the size of type, and the number of words or characters per line. One or more of these variables is usually given, or is unavoidable, simplifying the other design decisions.

Type for extended reading shouldn't be smaller than 9 point, and not larger than 14 point. Point size is a fairly arbitrary measurement (see page 53), so these suggestions are valid only for "normal" book typefaces – types with a very pronounced, or a very small x-height need to be carefully evaluated.

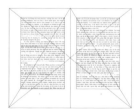
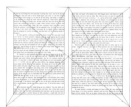

The arrangements, or layouts of our livingrooms still follow the same model they did generations ago. There is usually a comfortable chair or two, perhaps a sofa to accommodate more than one person, a table, a book-shelf, some lights. The only recent addition to this harmonious ensemble was the television set, which took over the center of attention from the oil painting on the wall.

Livingrooms, as opposed to bedrooms, serve a multitude of functions. Families sit together, and when they're not all staring in the same direction watching TV, they might actually play games at the table, eat dinner (all staring in the same direction), or even pursue individual interests such as reading, conversing, or staring in the same direction.

Certain types of books are used the same way: you can read, browse, look at pictures, or even check on something of particular interest. Pages offer various levels of entry for readers, viewers, and occasional browsers. These books will have to look different from our time-honored tomes of linear reading, just as livingrooms look different from bedrooms.

Some books look like catalogs, some like magazines. Some have the structure of a typical novel, but with illustrations, either integrated into the text or on separate pages. The reader is likely to peruse this sort of book in a more casual fashion, so the designer needs to provide several levels of typographic elements to act as guides through text and images.

If it has to be larger to accommodate pictures, or to provide room for text set in more than one column, a book most likely will have to be set down on a table to be studied rather than read. This means the margins can be smaller (no room needed for fingers to hold it) and that pictures can even extend to the edges of pages.

While books with only one level of copy usually need only one typeface in one size plus italic and small caps, more specialized books (such as this one) have to distinguish among the main text and other elements. This could mean a pronounced difference in type size; or perhaps another typeface with contrasting design, weight, or another color. In this book, we've employed a few of these levels at the same time.

If the contents, the illustrations, and the amount of copy vary from page to page, a flexible grid is needed. The one in this book allows for many different column widths, captions, and sidebars. These elements shouldn't be changed randomly on every other page, but when they do have to be adapted to varying contents, the underlying grid structure serves as a common denominator.

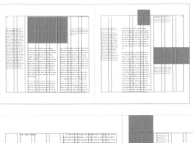

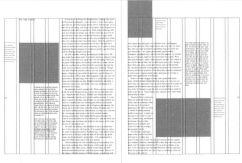

Hotel lobbies are institutional living-rooms. Guests and visitors spend time there doing what they might do at home, but in the company of strangers. The dress has to be more formal and one's attention is more likely to be distracted by the things going on, and the general level of activity rules out listening to one's personal choice of music. There is still the opportunity, however, for all to sit staring in the same direction and watch TV.

Some people manage to read real books in quasi-public places like hotel lobbies, but most spend their time there waiting for someone or something, so all they get to read is magazines. Magazine pages are designed for the casual reader: there are snippets of information or gossip (or one dressed up as the other), headlines, captions, and other graphic signposts pointing toward various tidbits of copy.

As advertisements change their look according to the latest typographic fashion, editorial pages tend to either look trendier, or deliberately stay sober and bookish.

Most magazines are printed in standard sizes; in the USA this means they're close to 8½ by 11 inches. A line of type needs to be at least six words (between 35 and 40 characters) long, so the type ought to be about 10 point to arrive at a column width of 55 to 60 mm, or 2¼ to 2⅜ inches. Three of these columns fit onto the page, leaving decent margins. The three-column grid is thus the basis for most publications printed on A4 paper, which is 8½ by 11 inches or 210 by 297 mm.

To allow for other elements besides the main text columns, these measurements have to be divided again. Captions can be set in smaller type and in very short lines, so they might fit into half a basic column, making it a six-unit grid.

A good way to make these grids more flexible and spontaneous is to leave one wide margin that would only occasionally be filled with type. This grid would then have an odd number of units, say seven or even thirteen. The more complex the contents, the more supple the grid has to be, allowing for different stories in different size types to occupy different widths.

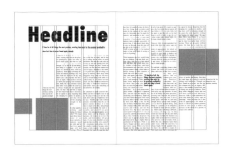

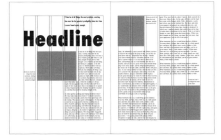

Kitchens are rooms with a clearly defined purpose: the storage, preparation, and often consumption of food and beverages. The equipment for these activities has changed considerably over the years and one could list numerous parallels to the development of typesetting systems over the same time span. The basic purpose has remained unchanged in both cases, whether it concerns food or type.

In a kitchen there are different surfaces for particular tasks, and containers and shelves for food, tools, crockery, pots, and pans. Graphic designers and typographers call the containers columns or picture boxes, the food is the text, the surface the page, and the tools are the typographic parameters needed to prepare an interesting page for the reader who has to digest it all.

Each recipe in a cookbook usually has explanatory text, a list of ingredients, and a step-by-step guide. It is sometimes illustrated either with small photographs or drawings. This sort of structure applies to any how-to publication, whether it's for car mechanics or landscapers.

People read cookbooks and other how-to manuals in situations that are often less than ideal. A cookbook has to compete for tabletop space with food, knives, towels, and bowls, and there is never enough time to read anything carefully. The text has to be read while standing, which means the type should be larger than usual. The recipe steps have to be clearly labeled with short headlines; ingredients and measurements have to be in lists that can be referred to at a glance.

The best – or worst – examples of badly designed information are found in instructions for mounting snowchains onto the wheels of your car. This operation is usually done in the dark when you're wet, in a hurry, and uncomfortably cold. The instructions are often printed on white paper, which, invariably gets wet and dirty before you've finished the job.

The typographic solution is to print them on the outside of the package, which should be made of some plastic material. The best color combination would be black type on a yellow background, which wouldn't show dirt as much as white. The type should be big and strong so it's legible no matter what. The text should be set in short, simple words and sentences.

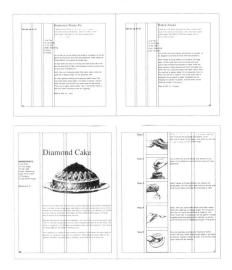

We spend much of our time outside our homes in places where our priorities are defined by other people. This is the case in most public places and, unfortunately, at work. Many people still have to work in conditions very much like this typing pool of the 1940s, even though it would be easy to improve the environment and thus the quality of work.

The same goes for much typographic work. There is no reason for hardworking pieces like price lists, technical catalogs, timetables, and similar heavy-duty information to look as ugly or complicated as they often do. If something looks dull, repetitive, and off-putting, people are going to approach it with a negative attitude (if they approach it at all). This does not improve their willingness to absorb the information.

Computers are a huge improvement over mechanical typewriters, and the output of laserprinters certainly looks much better than anything that ever came out of a typewriter. To create good visual communication, however, takes much more than good tools. Whenever you come across those official-looking, unreadable pieces, don't blame it on the equipment.

Complex information like price lists and timetables cannot be designed on a preconceived grid. The page arrangement has to come from the content and structure of the information itself. First you have to find the shortest and the longest elements, and then ignore them; if your layout accommodates the extremes you will end up making allowances for a few isolated exceptions. The thing to do is make the bulk of the matter fit, then go back to the exceptions and work with them one by one. If there are only a few long lines in an otherwise short listing, it should be considered an opportunity to flex your creative muscles: design around them or rewrite.

A sure way to improve the look and function of any information-intensive document is to eliminate boxes. Vertical lines are almost always unnecessary. Type creates its own vertical divisions along the lefthand edges of columns as long as there is sufficient space between columns. A vertical line is wasteful because it needs precious space on either side. Use space to divide elements from each other. Utilize horizontal lines to accentuate areas of the page. The edge of the paper makes its own box and doesn't need more boxes inside it.

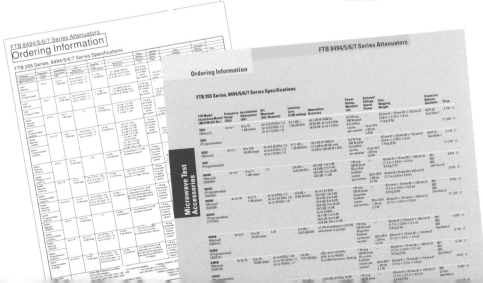

Now that your wife has bought
you a new suit, I don't mind
starting up a correspondence.

Groucho Marx (1895–1977)
was a member of the Marx
Brothers, one of the funniest
comedy teams in movie history.
In movies like *Horse Feathers*
and *Duck Soup*, Groucho is
perpetually punning while
displaying an incredible
facility for the leering look.

There is no bad type

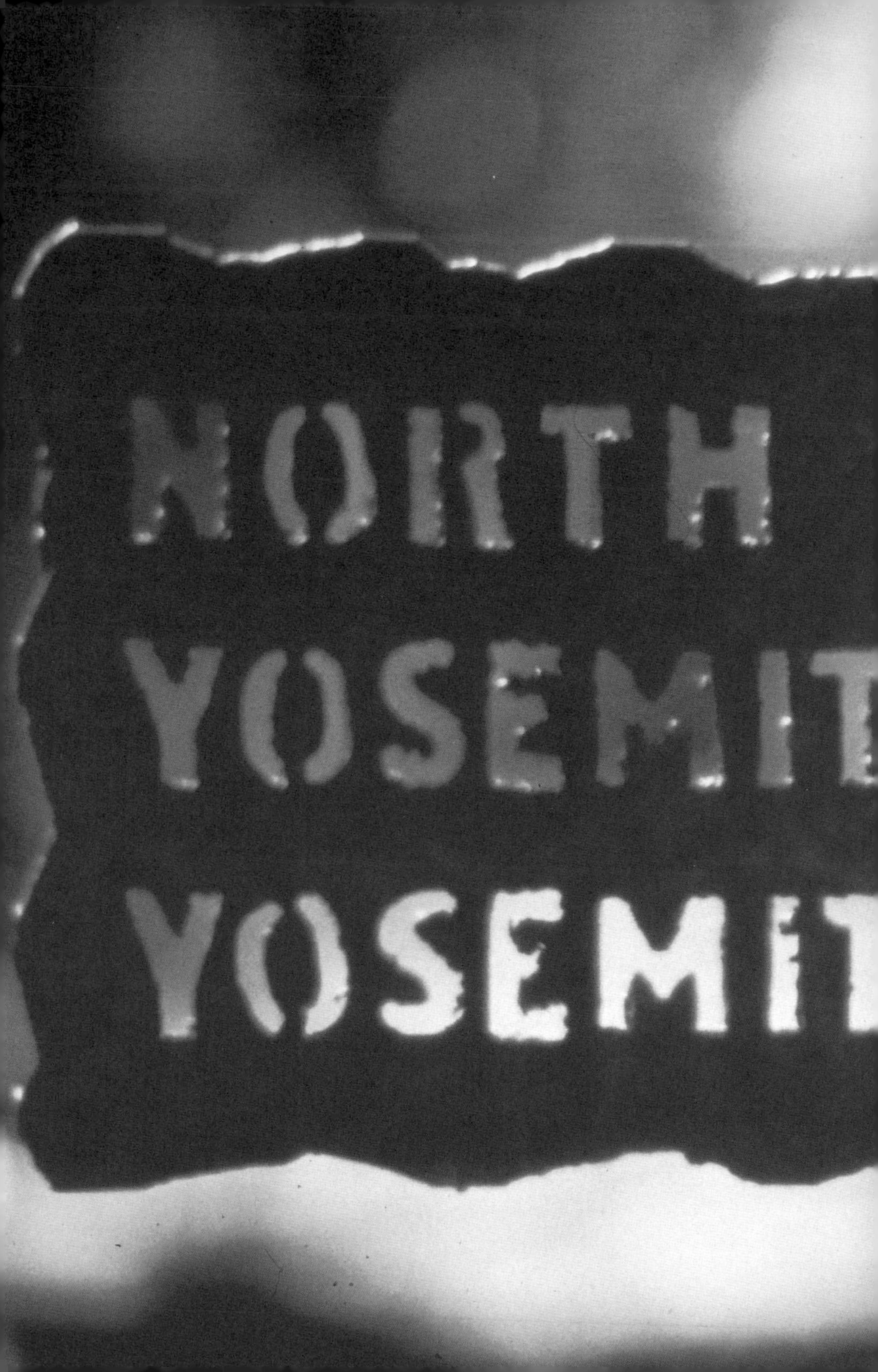
NORTH
YOSEMIT
YOSEMIT

From Mediterranean merchants making notes on clay tablets, to Roman masons chiseling letters into stone, to mediaeval monks moving quills across parchment – the look of letters has always been influenced by the tools used to make them. Two hundred years ago copperplate engraving changed the look of typefaces as did all subsequent technologies: the pantograph, Monotype and Linotype machines, phototypesetting, digital bitmaps, and outline fonts.

Most of these technologies are no longer viable, but some of the typefaces they engendered now represent particular categories in type classifications. Once again, the best example is the typewriter. As an office machine it is all but dead, but its typeface style survives as a typographic stereotype. Other recognizable typeface styles that have outlived their production methods are stenciled letters and constructed letters made with a square and compass.

Technical constraints no longer exist when it comes to the reproduction or re-creation of fonts from any and all periods. What used to be a necessity has become a look, just like pre-washed jeans are supposed to make everybody look like a cowboy who's been out on the trail for a few months.

Designers have gotten good mileage out of the low-tech look. Theoretically, almost every typeface could be stenciled; all it takes is a few lines to connect the inside shapes to the outside so the letters won't fall apart when cut out of metal.

At almost the same time two designers had the clever idea of creating a stencil typeface. Stencil, designed by R. Hunter Middleton was released in June of 1937; in July of that same year, Stencil, designed by Gerry Powell, was released.

Other typefaces also derive their style from the very absence of subtleties inherent in classic typefaces, for instance, the Italian architectural typeface styles exemplified in Eurostile, designed in 1962 by Aldo Novarese. Neville Brody's 1990 typeface, Insignia, at first looks like a crudely done mixture of Futura and Akzidenz Grotesk, but develops a certain rugged charm when it is used cleverly.

A true trend came out of Berkeley, California. Zuzana Licko of Emigre Graphics was inspired by the primitive bitmap fonts generated by the first Macintosh computers. She designed her own types within those constraints and they still look innovative today.

Almost twenty years ago someone at International Typeface Corporation realized that people wanted "honest" typewriter faces, but with all the benefits of "real" type. Joel Kaden and Tony Stan designed ITC American Typewriter, which answers all those needs.

.HANDGLOVES
STENCIL

.Handgloves
EUROSTILE

.Handgloves
INSIGNIA

.Handgloves
OAKLAND FIFTEEN

.Handgloves
ITC AMERICAN TYPEWRITER

If handwriting is done quickly, chances are the letter shapes in a word will be connected. Every stop, start, and pen lift of the writing hand slows down the process. Neon signs and cursive fonts work hand in hand, so to speak.

Neon tubes are filled with gas; the more interruptions there are in the continuous loop, the more expensive making the sign becomes. Signmakers therefore have to look for typefaces that connect as many letters as possible, or they must manipulate other types to accommodate the technical constraints.

The neon-sign style, in turn, influenced graphic design, and people have spent a lot of time airbrushing a glow of light around curved, tubular letters. Like other graphic manipulations, achieving neon effects has become much easier with drawing and painting programs available on the computer.

Signmakers working with neon take pride in their ability to select any old typeface and reproduce it in glass tubes. Because neon messages are generally short, the signmaker will most likely take the entire word and make into one shape. Even if inspiration comes from available type styles, the glass literally has to be bent and shaped to fit the design and technical requirements.

Since most signs are original designs, there hasn't been much call for real neon typefaces, although some fonts with glowing shadows and curvy shapes exist on transfer lettering. Some typefaces look as though they could be useful for neon signs. They have strokes of identical thickness throughout and no sharp angles or swelling of curves. Kaufmann fulfills these criteria and possesses some of that 1930s elegance.

The warm glow of the tube is created with the help of Adobe Photoshop.

.*Handgloves*

KAUFMANN

Handgloves

149

We associate particular typeface looks with certain products. Fresh produce always seems to want an improvised, handwritten sort of message, while high-tech demands a cool, technocratic look. Warm, cuddly products respond to a soft serif treatment, grainy whole foods are represented best by a handmade, rough-edged typeface, and serious money businesses like to recall the era of copperplate engraving, when deals were confirmed with a handshake.

In some cases this makes perfect sense. In city produce and meat markets where prices change constantly, time and expense prevents shopkeepers from having new signs printed each day. The most common solution is to write them out by hand; however, if the proprietor has illegible handwriting, it would be a disservice to customers to present an up-to-date but unreadable sign. The shopkeeper could simply buy a casual script or a brush font and print the signs reversed out on the laserprinter. They will look almost like genuine handwriting on a blackboard.

Advertising, especially in newspapers, has always tried to emulate the spontaneous style of small-time shopkeepers and their signwriters. There were plenty of brushstroke typefaces available in hot metal days, even though the immediacy of brushstrokes and the rigidity of metal letters seem to be a contradiction. Many brushstroke typefaces now exist in digital form.

The names signal their potential applications: Brush Script and Reporter are the rough, brushstroke typefaces; Charme and Present Script are more upscale. Mistral, the most spontaneous design of them all, has already been praised in this book (see page 45).

With a little determination and a lot of software savvy, all of us today can make fonts. Some of these homemade fonts, sold by independent digital foundries, have recently become very popular. Among them are FF Erikrighthand, designed by Erik van Blokland, and FF Justlefthand by Just van Rossum, which began as practical jokes.

Which one of these signs would you trust?

FRESH EGGS

Flying lessons

Fresh eggs

Flying lessons

.Handgloves

BRUSH SCRIPT

.Handgloves

REPORTER

.Handgloves

CHARME

.Handgloves

PRESENT SCRIPT

.Handgloves

FF ERIKRIGHTHAND

.Handgloves

FF JUSTLEFTHAND

FAX Message

Frugal INC. TIME MANAGEMENT

FRUGAL INC. TIME MANAGEMENT, 12 LATE STREET, KRONOS CITY, PM FAX 434 5369

To
The Timesavers/B.Franklin,
Savings Dept.
Cookoo's Clock-Street 9-5
Minnesota, 34 567 89,

From: Joe X. Ample

Date: 9.9.1999

No. of Pages

REGARDING Time Management

Dear Sirs,

Of all things we worked on lately, it appears that time was the most cost-intensive. Regarding that, we should not waste any of the company's precious resources. Fourty-five years of business experience indicate that wasted time is very hard to re-coup, as the statements at the end of the fiscal year always prove.

My proposal on this matter would be to intensify our efforts in the manufacturing field. We can not afford any delay; it would complicate the entire process. Instead, a hard-working industry would simplify many issues. Managers that arrive late in the morning will not be tolerated any longer. They hardly keep up with other, more efficient staff members.

It also shows that an inefficient and lengthy process costs more in time/money-terms than the actual manpower invested.

So what could be improved to avoid recession? We cannot make these times better it.... to wish for better times if we work hard m....

FAX Message

Frugal INC. TIME MANAGEMENT

FRUGAL INC. TOLL MANAGEMENT, 12 LATE STREET, KRONOS CITY, PM FAX 434 5369

From: Joe X. Ample

Date: 0 9 0 9 9 9

No. of Pages: 0 3
(Including this one)

To:
The Timesavers/B. Frank
Savings Dept
Cookoo's Clock-Street 9-5
Minnesota, 34 567 89

In Case of incomplete transmission please call 1-800-F A X B A C K

Regarding:
Time Management

Dear John,

Of all things we worked on lately, it appears that time was the most cost-intensive. Regarding that, we should not waste any of the company's precious

The letter is still the most common form of written business communication. Letterheads make the first impression and so are frequently printed on expensive, heavy paper in several colors, sometimes with blind embossing or mock steel engraving.

Then what happens? The letter is followed by a proposal, a memo, or another letter. After the initial exchange, it seems appropriate to just send a fax. After this message has been subjected to the tortuous process of sending and receiving, color, nice paper, and beautiful, legible type become a thing of the past. No one in business could live without a fax machine anymore, but even a fax message should be good looking and legible.

For faxing, choose a sturdy, well-defined typeface (no delicate shapes here). The type has to withstand the rigors of the faxing procedure; this means it is scanned and then printed at a modest resolution of 200 dpi (dots per inch) after already having been distorted during transmission. Most types with a background in typewriter technology, Letter Gothic and Courier, for instance, don't work very well for faxing. Neither do those types we use for book settings, such as Caslon or Garamond, unless they're set in at least 14 point.

Other things to avoid are heavy lines and boxes (they get distorted); small type (smaller than 9 point); heavy rules to write on (they end up obscuring the very handwriting they are supposed to clarify); and type at the very bottom of the page (because it makes the machine scan all the way down to the bottom, even if you have only written a short message). Try using a few symbols to brighten things up: telephone icons, arrows to denote "to" and "from," a little house for the address, and hands or triangles as pointers or bullets.

Frugalfax

← **Frugal Inc.**
Joe X. Ample
Time Management,
22 Late Street,
Kronos City, PM 34 567 89
✆ (434) 53 69 56

→ **The Timesavers Corp.**
B.Franklin,
Savings Dept.
Cookoo's Clock-Street 9-5
Minnesota, 34 567 89,
✆ (444) 55 05 45

Fax: (434) 53 69 45   Fax: (444) 55 05 40

☞ **Time Management**   Kronos City
                                          19. May 1992

Dear Sirs,

Of all the things we have worked on lately, it appears that time was the most cost-intensive. Regarding that, we should not waste any of the company's precious resources. Forty-five years of business experience indicate that wasted time is very difficult to re-coup, as the statements at the end of the fiscal year invariably prove.
    My proposal on this matter would be to intensify our efforts in the manufacturing field. We cannot afford any delay as it would complicate the entire process. Instead, a hardworking corporation would simplify most issues. Managers who arrive late in the morning will not be tolerated any longer; they hardly keep up with other, more efficient staff members. It also shows that inefficient and lengthy processes cost more in time/money-terms than the actual manpower invested.
    So what could be improved to avoid recession? We cannot make these times better if we ignore financial restraints. Our industry does not have to wish for better times if we work hard. Running the business on hope will only lead to quick bankruptcy.

Best Regards

Joe X. Ample
Vice President   1st. page of 4

.**Handgloves**
LUCIDA

.**Handgloves**
ITC STONE INFORMAL

.**Handgloves**
FRUTIGER 55

.**Handgloves**
PMN CAECILIA

153

Fru

The Timesa
Savings De
Cookoo's C
Minnesota,

DATE: 9. 9. 1999
TIME: 1:55 p.m.
TO: The Timesavers/B.Franklin
FROM: Joe X. Ample

Dear Sirs,

...ings we have worked on lately,
...intensive. Regarding
...precious re
...te t

Frugal Inc. Time Management, 12 Late Street, Kronos City, MN. 34567

Frugal
Incorporate

MEMO:

TIME: 9. 9. 1999
DATE: 1:55 p.m.
TO: The Timesavers/B.Franklin
FROM: Joe X. Ample

The Timesavers/B.Franklin,
Savings Dept.
Cookoo's Clock-Street 9-5
Minnesota, 3456789

Dear Sirs,

Of all the things we have worked on lately, it appears that time was the most
cost-intensive. Regarding that, we should not waste any of the company's
precious resources. Forty-five years of business experience indicate that
wasted time is very difficult to re-coup , as the statements at the end of the
fiscal year invariably prove.
My proposal on this matter would be to intensify our efforts in the manufacturing field . We cannot afford any delay; as it would complicate the entire
process. Instead, a hard-working corporation would simplify many issue
...anagers who arrive late in the morning will not be tol...
...ey hardly keep up with other, more effici...
...also shows that inst...
...e/mo...

Frugal
Incorporated

Time Management
12 Late Street
Kronos City, MN. 345678

The Timesavers/B.Franklin
Cookoo's Clock-Street 9-5
Kronos City, Minnesota 3456789

Memo

▶ The Timesavers/B.Franklin
◀ Joe X. Ample

Re-evaluating our progress

October 9. 1999
1:55 p.m.

Dear Sirs,

Of all the things we have worked on lately, it appears that time was the most cost-intensive. Regarding that, we should not waste any of the company's precious resources. Forty-five years of business experience indicate that wasted time is very difficult to re-coup , as the statements at the end of the fiscal year invariably prove.

My proposal on this matter would be to intensify our efforts in the manufacturing field . We cannot afford any delay; as it would complicate the entire process. Instead, a hard-working corporation would simplify many issues. Managers who arrive late in the morning will not be tolerated any longer; they hardly keep up with other, more efficient staff members. It also shows that inefficient and lengthy processes cost more in time/money-terms than the actual manpower invested.

So what could be improved to avoid recession? We cannot make these times better if we ignore our responsibility.

• Regarding our meeting scheduled for next Wednesday the 4th, please bring your new product for our time analysts to review.

Most of what's been said about faxes also applies to memos. However, because memos are not normally subjected to scanning and transmission over a wire, you can use types that are more delicate. In fact, most typefaces used for books, newspapers, and magazines look fine when printed on a good laserprinter, as long as the type is not too small.

You might want to get across that "old" office feel of the typewriter and its no-nonsense look. Try any of the sturdy-serif fonts – Corona, Glypha, Egyptienne F – or choose a cool matter-of-fact typeface like Formata, Bell Gothic, or Imago. If you want a traditional look, use Concorde, Utopia, or Versailles.

The rules of legibility also apply to memos. Make sure your lines are fairly short (the optimum is ten words), and put a narrow column next to the main message for headings and identification. The first things your correspondent should see are: who the memo is *to*, who it is *from*, *what* it is about, and *when* it was written.

.Handgloves
CORONA

.Handgloves
GLYPHA

.Handgloves
EGYPTIENNE F

.Handgloves
FORMATA

.Handgloves
BELL GOTHIC BOLD

.Handgloves
IMAGO BOOK

.Handgloves
CONCORDE

.Handgloves
UTOPIA

.Handgloves
VERSAILLES

155

1223	567
3445	564
6786	877
0034	651
2481	283
3274	000
2198	436
0004	765
7834	263
1223	567
3445	564

6786	007887	786878
3434	651200	766393

76876	886	342342
56464	687	788787
24234	003	2344

8	578	347	b
56		5	
73	6247	3	
53	48		
9492		9	
548	9765	2	7
6752	9	87	
358	9436	757	
85	1678	6	
76	125	4	6
723	5	1754	7
6541	276	87	
	48	1	
65	71	7136	
51	8	6578	6
57	87864	5	
8	76	58	
6	158		
763	565	5762	2
1	6	74	3
4	890		9

7236	4437	98	75986
		753247	652314
9823418	76872371	6675	
2347653	4276542	3786	
876	2389734	278652	34
786523	78	5642	387
423874	2376542	3786	5
4237983	419	875	67812
65167257	69561		
234896	234876	423	87642
3874		878	234897
509	450	971	0913
490	72		
3487	6751	765234	7654
376542	376653	4587	64876
42317863	4287	2187	
6456458	74	58764587	23874
13876		4378	
901008	9364589	80	3413
483462	34675	324	
765231	4	9823418	97
6872	37166	752347	34276

NTH		1	2				
LARIES		8000	8500				
INGE BENEFITS AND TAXES		2300	2300				
NT		4600	0				
SURANCE							
AVELING		900	900	900	900	900	90
EIGHT/MAI		200	200	200	200	200	2
PAIR		100	100	100	100	100	1
ASING MACH		0					
LEPHONE		500					
FICE SUPPL		3000					
URNALS		100					
GAL AND AC		5000					
NK CHARGES		50					
OTOCOPIES		0					
TOMOBILES		0					
VERTISING		3000					
NSULTING F		0					
HER		100					
CURITY		600					
M		28950					

Financial Statement
December 31, 1993

Assets

Current Assets		
Cash	1,000	
Accounts Receivable	3,000	
Notes Receivable	1,500	
Merchandise Inventory		4
Office Supplies		
Store Supplies		
Prepaid Insurance		
Total Current Assets		4
Plant Assets		
Land	5,000	
Buildings		7
Less Accumulated		
Depreciation	3,000	7
Store Equipment		2
Less Accumulated		
Depreciation	6,000	1
Total Plant Assets		9
Investments		5
Patents		1
Good Will	5,000	

Financial Statement
December 31, 1993

Assets

Current Assets

Cash	21,456		
Accounts Receivable	33,789		
Notes Receivable	31,012		
Merchandise Inventory		240,234	
Office Supplies	41,345		
Store Supplies	52,678		
Prepaid Insurance		323,567	
Current Assets		446,890	

Plant Assets

Land	65,902		
Buildings			276,123
Less Accumulated		345,567	
Depreciation	73,234	273,456	
Store Equipment			320,789
Less Accumulated	23,456		

Financial Statement
December 31, 1993

Assets

Current Assets

Cash	21,456		
Accounts Receivable	33,789		
Notes Receivable	31,012		
Merchandise Inventory		240,234	
Office Supplies	41,345		
Store Supplies	52,678		
Prepaid Insurance		323,567	
Current Assets		446,890	

Plant Assets

Land	65,902		
Buildings			276,123
Less Accumulated		345,567	
Depreciation	73,234	273,456	
Store Equipment			320,789
Less Accumulated	23.456		

Financial Statement
December 31, 1993

Assets

Current Assets

Cash	21,456		
Accounts Receivable	33,789		
Notes Receivable	31,012		
Merchandise Inventory		240,234	
Office Supplies	41,345		
Store Supplies	52,678		
Prepaid Insurance		323,567	
Current Assets		446,890	

Plant Assets

Land	65,902		
Buildings			276,123
Less Accumulated		345,456	
Depreciation	73,234	273,456	
Store Equipment			320,789
Less Accumulated			
Depreciation		436,123	414,345
Plant Assets	34,345	945,234	

Spreadsheets – as the name implies – need a lot of space. If you set them in Courier, you will end up with type that is small, and very easy to misread.

There are numbers that save space and that are still more legible than Helvetica or Times or those in your standard word processor font. Figures in tables have to be the same width or they will not line up properly in columns. Lining figures (numbers that don't have ascenders and descenders) are usually tabular and so do a reasonable job in this situation; lining figures are standard in most modern digital fonts.

For maximum legibility with added space economy, look at narrower than normal typefaces like News Gothic, or at condensed versions like Univers 57, Concorde Nova, and Frutiger Condensed. These types will set your spreadsheets apart from the norm: not only will they look better, but they will read better.

· 1234567890
News Gothic

· 1234567890
Univers 57

· 1234567890
Concorde Nova

· 1234567890
Frutiger Condensed

SCHRIFTGIESSEREI

JULIUS KLINKHARDT, LEIPZIG — WIEN

Stereotypie
Galvanoplastik
Chemitypie
Xylographische
Anstalt

→ Zierschriften ←

Nr. 385. **Tertia** (16 Punkte).

Jahresbericht Sigurds Brautfahrt

Poetisches Gedenkbuch 78 Deutsches Frauenleben

Einladung Amerikanische Reisestudien

2 Moniteur de l'Imprimerie 4

Stiftungs-Fest Tafelkarte Lieder-Abend

8   1   2   3   4   5   6   7   9

Nr. 386. **Text** (20 Punkte).

16 Lehrmittel-Ausstellung 39

Original Designing Trade Catalogues

Romane Lebensbilder Novellen

Spielbuch 58 Universum

Widmung Gesang-Verein Festgruss

8   1   2   3   4   5   6   7   9

No matter what turns technology takes, the typefaces we see most will still be those based upon letterforms from the end of the fifteenth century; the original Venetian or German models are evident in the diverse interpretations of every type designer since then. Garamond, Caslon, Baskerville, Bodoni; Gill, Zapf, Dwiggins, Frutiger: they all found inspiration in the past for typeface designs that were appropriate for their times and their tools. Every new imaging technology (as we call it today) results in a new generation of type designs. Today, outline fonts can emulate any shape imaginable, if not necessarily desirable; they can equal and even improve upon every aesthetic and technical refinement ever dreamed of or achieved.

Apart from the typefaces that work well because we are familiar with them, there are those that defy the simplistic classifications of usefulness or purpose. They may exist only because the type designer's first thought one morning was a new letter shape. These private artistic expressions may not appeal to a wide audience, but every now and again the right singer effortlessly transforms a simple song into a great hit. There are typographic gems hidden in today's specimen books just waiting to be discovered. In the right hands, technical constraints turn into celebrations of simplicity, and awkward alphabets are typographic heroes for a day.

There is no bad type.

This was new, modern, beautiful type in 1886. Later generations called the nineteenth century the "worst period in typographic history;" today we again admire the nostalgic charm of these decorative typefaces.

It takes time for a typeface to progress from concept through production to distribution, and from there to the type user's awareness. Typefaces are indicators of our visual and thus, cultural climate; type designers, therefore, have to be good at anticipating future trends. No amount of marketing will get a typeface accepted if it runs against the spirit of the time, whatever that may be.

Every once in a while a typeface is revived by graphic designers and typographers who dust it off and display it in new environments either as a reaction against prevailing preferences or simply because they want to try something different. Actual problem-solving often seems not to matter when it comes to choosing typefaces. True classic typefaces, that is, those with the beauty and proportion of their fifteenth-century ancestors, still win awards in the most chic and modern design annuals.

There is no bad type.

When you get to the fork in the road, take it.

Yogi Berra (1925–), Hall-of-Fame catcher for the New York Yankees, was one of the great all-time clutch hitters and a notorious bad ball hitter. Berra, who later managed the Yankees, has a natural ability to turn ordinary thoughts into linguistic ringers.

CHAPTER 10

Final form

Bibliography

Learning to use type properly might take a lifetime, but a lifetime of fun. In case you have now been bitten by the typographic bug, here is what we recommend as further reading on the subject. The list is far from complete, but includes both practical manuals and classic works. Some of these books are out of print, but can be found with a little effort in good used-book stores.

BIGELOW, CHARLES, PAUL HAYDEN DUENSING, LINNEA GENTRY. *Fine Print On Type: The Best of Fine Print on Type and Typography.* San Francisco: Fine Print /Bedford Arts, 1988.

BLUMENTHAL, JOSEPH. *The Printed Book in America.* Boston: David R. Godine, 1977.

BRINGHURST, ROBERT. *The Elements of Typographic Style.* Point Roberts, Washington: Hartley & Marks, 1992.

CARTER, SEBASTIAN. *Twentieth Century Type Designers.* New York: Taplinger Publishing Company, 1987.

CHAPPELL, WARREN. *A Short History of the Printed Word.* New York: Alfred A. Knopf, 1970.

The Chicago Manual of Style. Chicago: The University of Chicago Press, 1982.

DAIR, CARL. *Design with Type.* Toronto and Buffalo: University of Toronto Press, 1967.

DOWDING, GEOFFREY. *Finer Points in the Spacing and Arrangement of Type.* Point Roberts, Washington: Hartley & Marks, 1993.

DWIGGINS, WILLIAM ADDISON. *Layout in Advertising.* New York: Harper and Brothers, 1948.

FRUTIGER, ADRIAN. *Type, Sign, Symbol.* Zurich: ABC Verlag, 1980.

GILL, ERIC. *An Essay on Typography.* Boston: David R. Godine, 1988.

GRAY, NICOLETE. *A History of Lettering: Creative Experiment and Letter Identity.* Boston: David R. Godine, 1986.

HARLING, ROBERT. *The Letter Forms and Type Designs of Eric Gill.* Boston: David R. Godine, 1977.

Hart's Rules for Compositors and Readers. London: Oxford University Press, 1967.

HLAVSA, OLDRIČH. *A Book of Type and Design.* New York: Tudor Publishing, 1960.

JASPERT, W. PINCUS, W. TURNER BERRY, A.F. JOHNSON. *The Encyclopedia of Type Faces.* New York: Blandford Press, 1986.

KELLY, ROB ROY. *American Wood Type 1828–1900.* New York: Van Nostrand Reinhold, 1969.

KINROSS, ROBIN. *Modern Typography: An Essay in Critical History.* London: Hyphen Press, 1992.

LAWSON, ALEXANDER. *Anatomy of a Typeface.* Boston: David R. Godine, 1990.

LAWSON, ALEXANDER. *Printing Types: An Introduction.* Boston: Beacon Press, 1971.

LEWIS, JOHN. *Anatomy of Printing: The Influence of Art and History on its Design.* New York: Watson Guptill, 1970.

McGREW, MAC. *American Metal Typefaces of the Twentieth Century.* New Castle, Delaware: Oak Knoll Books, 1993.

McLEAN, RUARI. *The Thames and Hudson Manual of Typography.* London and New York: Thames and Hudson, 1980.

McLEAN, RUARI. *Jan Tschichold: Typographer.* Boston: David R. Godine, 1975.

MERRIMAN, FRANK. *A.T.A. Type Comparison Book.* New York: Advertising Typographers Association of America, 1965.

MORISON, STANLEY. *First Principles of Typography.* New York: The Macmillan Company, 1936.

MORISON, STANLEY. *A Tally of Types.* Cambridge: Cambridge University Press, 1973.

ROGERS, BRUCE. *Paragraphs on Printing.* New York: Dover Publication, 1979.

TRACY, WALTER. *Letters of Credit: A View of Type Design.* London: Gordon Fraser, 1986.

TSCHICHOLD, JAN. *The Form of the Book: Essays on the Morality of Good Design.* Point Roberts, Washington: Hartley & Marks, 1991.

TSCHICHOLD, JAN. *Alphabets and Lettering: A Source Book of the Best Letter Forms of Past and Present for Sign Painters, Graphic Artists, Typographers, Printers, Sculptors, Architects, and Schools of Art and Design.* Ware, Hertfordshire, England: Omega Books, 1985.

WILLIAMSON, HUGH. *Methods of Book Design: The Practice of an Industrial Craft.* New Haven and London: Yale University Press, 1985.

UPDIKE, DANIEL BERKELEY. *Printing Types: Their History, Forms, and Use.* Two Volumes. New York: Dover Publications, 1980.

Typeface index

Metro William Addison Dwiggins, 1930: **132**

Minion™ **multiple master** Robert Slimbach, 1992: **21, 101, 111, 130**

Mistral® Roger Excoffon, 1955: **45, 151**

F Moonbase Alpha Cornel Windlin, 1991: **33**

Myriad™ Robert Slimbach & Carol Twombly, 1992: **21, 63, 91, 101, 109**

Neue Helvetica* Linotype Corporation, 1983: **79, 103, 105, 107**

News Gothic Morris Fuller Benton, 1908: **63, 157**

Oakland Fifteen Zuzana Licko, 1985: **147**

OCR B Adrian Frutiger, 1968: **19, 67**

ITC Officina™ Erik Spiekermann, 1990: **19**

Palatino* Hermann Zapf, 1952: **61**

Perpetua Eric Gill, 1925: **88**

Poetica™ Robert Slimbach, 1992: **51**

Poplar™ Kim Buker, Barbara Lind & Joy Redick, 1990: **49, 85**

Present Script* Friedrich Karl Sallwey, 1974: **151**

Reporter® C. Winkow, 1953: **151**

Rockwell® F. H. Pierpont, 1934: **43**

Agfa Rotis™ Otl Aicher, 1989: **101**

Runic Condensed™ Monotype Corporation, 1935: **43**

Sabon* Jan Tschichold, 1966: **51**

Sassoon Primary® Rosemary Sassoon, 1990: **37**

Stempel Schneidler® F. H. E. Schneidler, 1936: **41, 59**

Serifa® Adrian Frutiger, 1967: **79**

Snell Roundhand* Matthew Carter, 1965: **39, 40, 65**

ITC Souvenir® Ed Benguiat, 1977: **41**

Spartan Classified® John Renshaw & Gerry Powell, 1939: **37**

Stencil Robert Hunter Middleton, June 1937: **147**

Stencil Gerry Powell, July 1937: **147**

ITC Stone® Sumner Stone, 1987: **19, 50, 63, 101, 153**

Stymie Saul Hess & Gerry Powell, 1935: **43**

Syntax* Hans-Eduard Meier, 1968: **47, 51**

Tekton™ David Siegel, 1990: **39, 40, 95**

Tempo™ Robert Hunter Middleton, 1940: **85**

Times New Roman® Stanley Morison & Victor Lardent, 1931: **57, 59, 61, 157**

Trajan™ Carol Twombly, 1989: **25**

Typo Upright American Type Founders, 1905: **43**

Univers* Adrian Frutiger 1957: **61, 75, 79, 103, 107, 157**

Universal News and Commercial Pi 51: 85

University of California Oldstyle Frederic Goudy, 1938: **81**

Utopia™ Robert Slimbach, 1989: **155**

VAG Rounded Volkswagen corporate typeface, 1976: **37**

Versailles* Adrian Frutiger, 1982: **155**

Berthold Walbaum™ Günter Gerhard Lange, 1976: **65**

ITC Weidemann® Kurt Weidemann, 1983: **37**

Weiss® Rudolf Weiss, 1926: **93**

Welt Ludwig & Mayer, 1930: **43**

Wilhelm Klingspor Gotisch™ Rudolf Koch, 1925: **51**

Index

Credits

 12 Newsstand

Photo: Gene Fitzer
© Superstock,
New York
Picture research:
Susan Friedman, S.F.

 16 Labels

Typographic design:
Thomas Nagel,
MetaDesign West

 18 Forms

Typographic design:
Thomas Nagel,
MetaDesign West

 6 Street sign
Stockholm

Photo:
Erik Spiekermann,
Berlin

 8 Paul Watzlawick

Quotation is public
domain

 10 Salt & Pepper

Photo:
Dennis Hearne,
San Francisco

11 Japanese sign
Photo:
Joel Sackett, Seattle

Cereal package:
Thomas Nagel,
MetaDesign West

 20 German
freeway signs

Photo:
Helmuth Langer,
Köln

 22 Tallulah
Bankhead

Quotation attributed
to Ms. Bankhead

 24 Trajan Column,
Rome

Photo: Victoria &
Albert Museum,
London

26
Hypnerotomachia
Poliphili

Photo:
Fred Brady

 27 Gutenberg bible

From the library of
Jack Stauffacher,
San Francisco

 28 Handwriting
samples

From the library of
Jack Stauffacher,
San Francisco

 30 Winter tree

Photo:
Peter de Lory,
San Francisco

 32 Typographic
Image Design:

Jeff Zwerner
MetaDesign West

 38-40 Shoes

Photos:
©Adobe Systems

 42 Doubt

Photo:
Dennis Hearne,
San Francisco
Actress:
Megan Bierman

 44 Surprise

Photo:
Dennis Hearne,
San Francisco
Actress:
Megan Bierman

46 Joy

Photo:
Dennis Hearne,
San Francisco
Actress:
Megan Bierman

48 Anger

Photo:
Dennis Hearne,
San Francisco
Actress:
Megan Bierman

52 Human face
Leonardo da Vinci

Photo©R. Gamm/
Superstock
Picture research:
Susan Friedman, S.F.

54 Gerry Mulligan

Quotation from a
radio interview: used
with permission of
National Public
Radio.

56 Packing to travel

Photo:
Peter de Lory,
San Francisco

58 Vacation

Photo:
Peter de Lory,
San Francisco

60 Business

Photo:
Peter de Lory,
San Francisco

62 Work

Photo:
Peter de Lory,
San Francisco

64 Formal

Photo:
Peter de Lory,
San Francisco

66 Trendy

Photo:
Peter de Lory,
San Francisco

67 Trendy types

Typographic design:
Thomas Nagel,
MetaDesign West

68 Sherlock Holmes

Quotation from
Beatrice Warde used
with permission of
the Typophiles, Inc.

70 The Way To
Wealth

Typographic design:
Jeff Zwerner,
MetaDesign West

72 Advertisement

Typographic design:
Jeff Zwerner,
MetaDesign West

74 New Wave

Typographic design:
MetaDesign West

76 Annual report

Typographic design:
Nancy Zeches,
MetaDesign West

78 Order form

Typographic design:
Jeff Zwerner,
MetaDesign West

80 Magazine

Typographic design:
Nancy Zeches,
MetaDesign West

82 Nostalgia

Typographic design:
MetaDesign West

84 Tabloid

Typographic design:
MetaDesign West

86 Symbols

Typographic design:
Thomas Nagel,
MetaDesign West

88 Eric Gill

Quotation used with permission of David R. Godine, Publishers

90 John, Paul, George & Rita

Photo:
Dennis Hearne,
San Francisco

92 John, Paul, George & Rita

Photo:
Dennis Hearne,
San Francisco

94 John, Paul, George & Rita

Photo:
Dennis Hearne,
San Francisco

96 The Trapp Family

© Wide World Photo
Picture research:
Susan Friedman,
San Francisco

98 Guitars

© Wide World Photo
Picture research:
Susan Friedman,
San Francisco

100 The Lawrence Welk Family

© The Bettman Archives
Picture research:
Susan Friedman, S.F.

102 The Flute Player
Adolph von Menzel

© Superstock
Picture research:
Susan Friedman,
San Francisco

104 Tuba player

© Photoworld/
FPG, Int.
Picture research:
Susan Friedman,
San Francisco

106 Metronome

Photo:
Dennis Hearne,
San Francisco

108 Philharmonic orchestra

© R. Llwellyn/
Superstock
Picture research:
Susan Friedman, S.F.

110 Small book

Photo:
Dennis Hearne,
San Francisco;
from the collection
of Joyce Lancaster
Wilson

112 Frederic Goudy

Quotation attributed
to Mr. Goudy

114 Tree farm

Photo:
Dennis Hearne,
San Francisco

116 Summer tree

Photo:
Peter de Lory,
San Francisco

118 Marathon runners

© P. Cantor/ Super-
stock
Picture research:
Susan Friedman, S.F.

120 Sprinter

© R.Llewellyn/
Superstock
Picture research:
Susan Friedman,
San Francisco

122 Freeway day-
time/road at night

© Richard H. Smith/
FPG, Int.
Picture research:
Susan Friedman, S.F.

124 Freeway
daytime

© Robert Bennett/
FPG, Int.
Picture research:
Susan Friedman, S.F.

126 City traffic

© Tony Stone
Worldwide
Picture research:
Susan Friedman,
San Francisco

128 Traffic jam

© Tony Stone
Worldwide
Picture research:
Susan Friedman,
San Francisco

129 Space

Typographic design:
Jeff Zwerner,
MetaDesign West

 144 Groucho Marx

Quotation used with
permission of
Simon & Schuster,
Publishers

 158 Type specimen

From the library of
Jack Stauffacher,
San Francisco

 132 William Addison
Dwiggins

Quote used with
permission of Harper
Collins, Publishers

 146 Yosemite park

Photo:
Lynne Garell,
Menlo Park

 160 Yogi Berra

Quotation attributed
to Mr. Berra

 134 Bedroom

Photo:
Dennis Hearne,
San Francisco

 148 Neon sign

Photo:
Peter de Lory,
San Francisco

 173 Thunder

Photo:
Patrick Ames

 136 Livingroom

© M. Helfer/
Superstock
Picture research:
Susan Friedman,
San Francisco

 150 Shop sign, Paris

Photo:
Erik Spiekermann,
Berlin

 138 Hotel lobby

Photo:
Hotel Triton,
San Francisco;
Dennis Hearne,
San Francisco

 152-153 Faxes

Typographic design:
Thomas Nagel
MetaDesign West

 140 Kitchen

© M. Helfer/
Superstock
Picture research:
Susan Friedman,
San Francisco

 154-155 Memos

Typographic design:
Jeff Zwerner
MetaDesign West

 142 Typing pool

© Historical Pictures/
Stock Montage
Picture research:
Susan Friedman,
San Francisco

 156-157
Spreadsheets

Typographic design:
Thomas Nagel,
MetaDesign West

Design, illustration, and production
>MetaDesign West, San Francisco, California.
Andrea Herstowski, Bill Hill, Terry Irwin,
Jens Kreitmeyer, Thomas Nagel, Erik
Spiekermann, Andrew Waegel, Tyler Wheeler,
Deborah Whitney, Nancy Zeches, Jeff Zwerner

Readers and type advisors
>Jocelyn Bergen, Elsie V. Brenner, Margery
Cantor, Burwell Davis, Molly S. Detwiler,
Ilene N. Ellickson, Lynne Garell, Alexander
Lawson, Mac McGrew, Will H. Powers,
Fritz Streiff, Carol Twombly

Editor in chief
>Patrick Ames

Cover design
>Jeff Zwerner & Erik Spiekermann

>Designed and produced using Adobe
Illustrator, Adobe Photoshop, and
QuarkXPress on Macintosh IIci and
Quadra 700 computers.

>Proofs were printed on an Apple LaserWriter
IIg and a Canon CLC 300 with an Adobe
PostScript RIP.

>Metagraphics, Palo Alto, California, created
scans and electronic duotones, and output
final film at 175 LPI using an Adobe/Scitex
PostScript RIP and Scitex Dolev imagesetter.

>Typefaces from the Adobe Type Library were
used throughout this book, with Myriad and
Minion multiple master as primary text fonts.

>Printed by Shepard Poorman, Indianapolis,
Indiana.